GUIDE TO PRAYER

GUIDE TO PRAYER

ISBN 1-58660-224-1

All Scripture quotations, unless otherwise noted, are taken from the King James Version of the Bible.

Published by Humble Creek, P.O. Box 719, Uhrichsville, Ohio 44683

Printed in the United States of America.

INTRODUCTION

Prayer, in its simplest definition, is talking with God. And whether our prayers are happy, sad, angry, or loving, whether they're done while kneeling, standing, or sitting, God is always listening, wanting to answer our requests in His perfect time.

Between the covers of this book, you'll find a *Guide to Prayer*—encouragement and inspiration for your own prayer life. Beginning with *A 31-Day Guide to Prayer* by the great Christian theologian Andrew Murray, you'll learn how to "pray without ceasing" (1 Thessalonians 5:17), what to pray for, and how to pray for it. Then in *Prayer Starters,* you'll encounter a collection of two hundred prayers arranged into fifty practical topics. These prayers will help you begin a vital prayer life of your own.

This indispensable guide to deeper and more meaningful prayer will lead you to a closer relationship with God and His Son Jesus Christ. Read on and experience the power of prayer.

A 31-Day Guide to Prayer

ANDREW MURRAY

PRAY WITHOUT CEASING

(A THIRTY-ONE DAY COURSE)

Pray without ceasing. Who can do this? How can one do it who is surrounded by the cares of daily life? How can a mother love her child without ceasing? How can the eyelid without ceasing hold itself ready to protect the eye? How can I breathe and feel and hear without ceasing? Because all these are the functions of a healthy, natural life. And so, if the spiritual life be healthy, under the full power of the Holy Spirit, praying without ceasing will be natural.

Pray without ceasing. Does it refer to continual acts of prayer, in which we are to persevere till we obtain, or to the spirit of prayerfulness that should animate us all the day? It includes both. The example of our Lord Jesus shows us this. We have to enter our closet for special seasons of prayer; we are at times to persevere there in importunate prayer. We are also all the day to walk in God's presence, with the whole heart set upon heavenly things. Without set times of prayer, the spirit of prayer will be dull and feeble. Without the continual prayerfulness, the set times will not avail.

Pray without ceasing. Does that refer to prayer for ourselves or others? To both. It is because many confine it to themselves that they fail so in practicing it. It is only when the branch gives itself to bear fruit, more fruit, much fruit, that it can live a healthy life and expect a rich inflow of sap. The death of Christ brought Him to the place of everlasting intercession. Your death with Him to sin and self sets you free from the care of self and elevates you to the dignity of intercessor—one who can get life and blessing from God for others. Know your calling; begin this your work. Give yourself wholly to it, and ere you know, you will be finding something of this *"Praying always"* within you.

Pray without ceasing. How can I learn it? The best way of learning to do a thing—in fact the only way—is *to do it.* Begin by setting apart some time every day, say ten or fifteen minutes, in which you say to God and to yourself, that you come to Him now as intercessor for others. Let it be after your morning or evening prayer, or any other time. If you cannot secure the same time every day, be not troubled.

Only see that you do your work. Christ chose you and appointed you to pray for others.

If at first you do not feel any special urgency or faith or power in your prayers, let not that hinder you. Quietly tell your Lord Jesus of your feebleness; believe that the Holy Spirit is in you to teach you to pray, and be assured that if you begin, God will help you. God cannot help you unless you begin and keep on.

Pray without ceasing. How do I know what to pray for? If once you begin and think of all the needs around, you will soon find enough. But to help you this little tract is issued, with subjects and hints for prayer for a month. It is meant that we should use it month by month, until we know more fully to follow the Spirit's leading, and have learned, if need be, to make our own list of subjects, and can dispense with it. In regard to the use of these helps, a few words may be needed.

1. How to pray. You notice for every day two headings—the one What to Pray; the other, How to Pray. If the subjects were only given, one might fall into the routine of mentioning names and things before God, and the work become a burden. The hints under the heading How to Pray are meant to remind of the spiritual nature of the work, of the need of divine help, and to encourage faith in the certainty that God, through the Spirit, will give us grace to pray aright, and will also hear our prayer. One does not at once learn to take his place boldly and to dare to believe that he will be heard. Therefore take a few moments each day to listen to God's voice reminding you of how certainly even you will be heard, and calling on you to pray in that faith in your Father to claim and take the blessing you plead for. And let these words about How to Pray enter your hearts and occupy your thoughts at other times, too. The work of intercession is Christ's great work on earth, entrusted to Him because He gave Himself the sacrifice to God for men, and the work will become your glory and your joy, too.

2. What to pray. Scripture calls us to pray for many things: for all saints; for all men; for kings and all rulers; for all who are in adversity; for the sending forth of laborers; for those who labor in the gospel; for all converts; or believers who have fallen into sin; for one another in our own immediate circles. The church is now so much larger than when the New Testament was written; the number of forms of work and workers is so much greater, the needs of the church and the world are so much better known, that we need to take time and thought to see where prayer is needed and to what our heart is most drawn out. The Scripture calls to prayer demand a large heart, taking in all saints and all men and all needs. An attempt has been made in these helps to indicate what the chief subjects are that need prayer and that ought to interest every Christian.

It will be felt difficult by many to pray for such large spheres as are sometimes mentioned. Let it be understood that in each case we may make special intercession for our own circle of interest coming under that heading. And it is hardly needful to say, further, that where one subject appears of more special interest or urgency than another we are free for a time day after day to take up that subject. If only time be really given to intercession, and the spirit of believing intercession be cultivated, the object is attained. While on the one hand, the heart must be enlarged at times to take in all, the more pointed and definite our prayer can be the better.

3. Answers to prayer. More than one little book has been published in which Christians may keep a register of their petitions and note when they were answered. When we pray for all saints or for missions in general, it is difficult to know when or how our prayer is answered, or whether our prayer has had any part in bringing the answer. It is of extreme importance that we should prove that God hears us, and to this end take note of what answers we look for and when they come. On the day of praying for all saints, take the saints in your congregation, or in your prayer meeting, and ask for a revival among them. Take, in connection with missions, some special station or missionary you are interested in, or more than one, and plead for blessing. And expect and look for its coming that you may praise God.

4. Prayer circles. There is no desire in publishing this invitation to intercession to add another to the many existing prayer unions or praying bands. The first object is to stir the many Christians who practically, through ignorance of their calling or unbelief as to their prayer availing much, take but very little part in the work of intercession; and then to help those who do pray to some fuller apprehension of the greatness of the work and the need of giving their whole strength to it. There is a circle of prayer which asks for prayer on the first day of every month for the fuller manifestation of the power of the Holy Spirit throughout the church. I have given the words of that invitation as subject for the first day, and taken the same thought as keynote all through. The more one thinks of the need and the promise and the greatness of the obstacles to be overcome in prayer, the more one feels it must become our lifework day by day, that to which every other interest is subordinated.

But while not forming a large prayer union, it is suggested that it may be found helpful to have small prayer circles to unite in prayer, either for one month, with some special object introduced daily along with the others, or through a year or longer, with the view of strengthening each other in the grace of intercession. If a minister were to invite some of his neighboring brethren to join for some special requests along with the printed subjects for supplication, or a number of the more earnest members of his congregation to unite in prayer for revival, some might be trained to take their place in the great work of intercession, who now stand idle because no man hath hired them.

5. Who is sufficient for these things? The more we study and try to practice this grace of intercession, the more we become overwhelmed by its greatness and our feebleness. Let every such impression lead us to listen: My grace is sufficient for thee and to answer truthfully: Our sufficiency is of God. Take courage; it is in the intercession of Christ you are called to take part. The burden and the agony, the triumph and the victory are all His. Learn from Him, yield to His Spirit in you to know how to pray. He gave Himself a sacrifice to God for men, that He might have the right and power of intercession. "He bare the sin of many, and made intercession for the transgressors." Let your faith rest boldly on His finished work. Let your heart wholly identify itself with Him in His death and His life. **Like Him,** give yourself to God a sacrifice for men: It is your highest nobility; it is your true and full union to Him; it will be to you, as to Him, your power of intercession. Beloved Christian! come and give your whole heart and life to intercession, and you will know its blessedness and its power. God asks nothing less; the world needs nothing less; Christ asks nothing less; let nothing less be what we offer to God.

Day One

WHAT TO PRAY: For the Power of the Holy Spirit

I bow my knees unto the Father. . .that he would grant you. . . to be strengthened with might by his Spirit.
Ephesians 3:14, 16

Wait for the promise of the Father.
Acts 1:4

The fuller manifestation of the grace and energy of the blessed Spirit of God, in the removal of all that is contrary to God's revealed will, so that we grieve not the Holy Spirit, but that He may work in mightier power in the church for the exaltation of Christ and the blessing of souls.

God has one promise to and through His exalted Son; our Lord has one gift to His church; the church has one need; all prayer unites in the one petition the power of the Holy Spirit. Make it your one prayer.

HOW TO PRAY: As a Child Asks a Father

If a son shall ask bread of any of you that is a father, will he give him a stone? . . . How much more shall your heavenly Father give the Holy Spirit to them that ask him?
Luke 11:11, 13

Ask as simply and trustfully as a child asks bread. You can do this because "God hath sent forth the Spirit of his Son into your hearts, crying, Abba, Father." This Spirit is in you to give you childlike confidence. In the faith of His praying in you, ask for the power of that Holy Spirit everywhere. Mention places or circles where you specially ask it to be seen.

Day Two

WHAT TO PRAY: For the Spirit of Supplication

The Spirit itself maketh intercession for us.
Romans 8:26

I will pour [out]. . .the spirit of. . .supplication.
Zechariah 12:10

Every child of God has the Holy Spirit in him to pray. God waits to give the Spirit in full measure. Ask for yourself, and all who join, the outpouring of the Spirit of supplication. Ask it for your own prayer circle.

HOW TO PRAY: In the Spirit

Praying always with all prayer and supplication in the Spirit.
Ephesians 6:18

Praying in the Holy Ghost.
Jude 20

Our Lord gave His disciples on His resurrection day the Holy Spirit to enable them to wait for the full outpouring on the day of Pentecost. It is only in the power of the Spirit already in us, acknowledged and yielded to, that we can pray for His fuller manifestation. Say to the Father, it is the Spirit of His Son in you that is urging you to plead His promise.

Day Three

WHAT TO PRAY: For all Saints

With all prayer and supplication in the Spirit, and watching thereunto with all perseverance and supplication for all saints.
Ephesians 6:18

Every member of a body is interested in the welfare of the whole and exists to help and complete the others. Believers are one body and ought to pray, not so much for the welfare of their own church or society, but, first of all, for all saints. This large, unselfish love is the proof that Christ's Spirit and love are teaching them to pray. Pray first for all and then for the believers around you.

HOW TO PRAY: In the Love of the Spirit

By this shall all men know that ye are my disciples, if ye have love one to another.
John 13:35

[I pray]. . .that they all may be one. . . that the world may believe that thou hast sent me.
John 17:20–21

I beseech you, brethren. . .for the love of the Spirit, that ye strive together with me in your prayers to God for me.
Romans 15:30

Above all things have fervent charity among yourselves.
1 Peter 4:8

If we are to pray we must love. Let us say to God we do love all His saints; let us say we love specially every child of His we know. Let us pray with fervent love, in the love of the Spirit.

Day Four

WHAT TO PRAY: For the Spirit of Holiness

God is the holy One. His people is a holy people. He speaks: I am holy: I am the Lord who makes you holy. Christ prayed: Sanctify them. Make them holy through Thy truth. Paul prayed: "[God] stablish your hearts unblameable in holiness." God of peace, sanctify you wholly!

Pray for all saints—God's holy ones—throughout the church that the Spirit of holiness may rule them. Specially for new converts. For the saints in your own neighborhood or congregation. For any you are specially interested in. Think of their special need, weakness, or sin; and pray that God may make them holy.

HOW TO PRAY: Trusting in God's Omnipotence

The things that are impossible with men are possible with God. When we think of the great things we ask for, of how little likelihood there is of their coming, of our own insignificance—prayer is not only wishing or asking, but believing and accepting. Be still before God and ask Him to give you to know Him as the almighty One, and leave your petitions with Him who doeth wonders.

Day Five

WHAT TO PRAY: That God's People May Be Kept from the World

Holy Father, keep through thine own name those whom thou hast given me. . . . I pray not that thou shouldest take them out of the world, but that thou shouldest keep them from the evil. They are not of the world, even as I am not of the world.

John 17:11, 15–16

In the last night Christ asked three things for His disciples: that they might be kept as those who are not of the world; that they might be sanctified; that they might be one in love. You cannot do better than pray as Jesus prayed. Ask for God's people that they may be kept separate from the world and its spirit; that they, by the Holy Spirit, may live as those who are not of the world.

HOW TO PRAY: Having Confidence before God

Beloved, if our heart condemn us not, then have we confidence toward God. And whatsoever we ask, we receive of him, because we keep his commandments, and do those things that are pleasing in his sight.

1 John 3:21–22

Learn these words by heart. Get them into your heart. Join the ranks of those who, with John, draw nigh to God with an assured heart that does not condemn them, having confidence toward God. In this spirit, pray for your brother who sins (1 John 5:16). In the quiet confidence of an obedient child, plead for those of your brethren who may be giving way to sin. Pray for all to be kept from the evil. And say often, "What we ask, we receive, because we keep and do."

Day Six

WHAT TO PRAY: For the Spirit of Love in the Church

[I pray] that they may be one, even as we are one:
I in them and thou in Me. . .that the world may know that
thou hast sent me, and hast loved them, as thou hast loved me. . .that
the love wherewith thou hast loved me may be in them,
and I in them.
John 17:22–23, 26

The fruit of the Spirit is love.
Galatians 5:22

Believers are one in Christ, as He is one with the Father. The love of God rests on them and can dwell in them. Pray that the power of the Holy Ghost may work this love in believers, that the world may see and know God's love in them. Pray much for this.

HOW TO PRAY: As One of God's Remembrancers

I have set watchmen upon thy walls. . .
which shall never hold their peace day nor night:
ye that make mention of the Lord keep not silence,
and give him no rest.
Isaiah 62:6–7

Study these words until your whole soul be filled with the consciousness, I am appointed intercessor. Enter God's presence in that faith. Study the world's need with that thought—it is my work to intercede; the Holy Spirit will teach me for what and how. Let it be an abiding consciousness: My great lifework, like Christ's, is intercession—to pray for believers and those who do not yet know God.

Day Seven

WHAT TO PRAY: For the Power of the Holy Spirit on Ministers

I beseech you. . .that ye strive together with me
in your prayers to God for me.
Romans 15:30

He will yet deliver us;
ye also helping together by prayer. . .on our behalf.
2 Corinthians 1:10–11

What a great host of ministers there are in Christ's church. What need they have of prayer. What a power they might be, if they were all clothed with the power of the Holy Ghost. Pray definitely for this; long for it. Think of your own minister, and ask it very specially for him. Connect every thought of the ministry, in your town or neighborhood or the world, with the prayer that all may be filled with the Spirit. Plead for them the promise, "Tarry. . .until ye be endued with power from on high." "Ye shall receive power, after that the Holy Ghost is come upon you."

HOW TO PRAY: In Secret

But thou, when thou prayest, enter into thy closet,
and when thou hast shut thy door, pray to thy Father which is in secret.
Matthew 6:6

He went up into a mountain apart to pray. . .he was there alone.
Matthew 14:23; see also John 6:15

Take time and realize, when you are alone with God: Here am I now, face-to-face with God, to intercede for His servants. Do not think you have no influence or that your prayer will not be missed. Your prayer and faith will make a difference. Cry in secret to God for His ministers.

Day Eight

WHAT TO PRAY: For the Spirit on All Christian Workers

Ye also helping together by prayer for us,
that for the gift bestowed upon us by the means
of many persons thanks may be given by many on our behalf.
2 Corinthians 1:11

What multitudes of workers in connection with our churches and missions, our railways and postmen, our soldiers and sailors, our young men and young women, our fallen men and women, our poor and sick. God be praised for this! What could they accomplish if each were living in the fullness of the Holy Spirit! Pray for them; it makes you a partner in their work, and you will praise God each time you hear of blessing anywhere.

HOW TO PRAY: With Definite Petitions

What wilt thou that I shall do unto thee?
Luke 18:41

The Lord knew what the man wanted, and yet He asked him. The utterance of our wish gives point to the transaction in which we are engaged with God, and so awakens faith and expectation. Be very definite in your petitions, so as to know what answer you may look for. Just think of the great host of workers, and ask and expect God definitely to bless them in answer to the prayers of His people. Then ask still more definitely for workers around you. Intercession is not the breathing out of pious wishes; its aim is, in believing, persevering prayer, to receive and bring down blessing.

Day Nine

WHAT TO PRAY: For God's Spirit on Our Mission Work

As they ministered to the Lord, and fasted, the Holy Ghost said, Separate me Barnabas and Saul. . . . When they had fasted and prayed, . . . they sent them away. So they, being sent forth by the Holy Ghost, departed.
Acts 13:2–4

The evangelization of the world depends first of all upon a revival of prayer. Deeper than the need for men—aye, deep down at the bottom of our spiritless life, is the need for the forgotten secret of prevailing, worldwide prayer.

Pray that our mission work may all be done in this spirit—waiting on God, hearing the voice of the Spirit, sending forth men with fasting and prayer. Pray that in our churches our mission interest and mission work may be in the power of the Holy Spirit and of prayer. It is a Spirit-filled, praying church that will send out Spirit-filled missionaries, mighty in prayer.

HOW TO PRAY: Take Time

I give myself unto prayer.
Psalm 109:4

We will give ourselves continually to prayer.
Acts 6:4

Be not rash with thy mouth,
and let not thine heart be hasty to utter any thing before God.
Ecclesiastes 5:2

And [He] continued all night in prayer to God.
Luke 6:12

Time is one of the chief standards of value. The time we give is a proof of the interest we feel.

We need time with God—to realize His presence; to wait for Him to make Himself known; to consider and feel the needs we plead for; to take our place in Christ; to pray 'til we can believe that we have received. Take time in prayer, and pray down blessing on the mission work of the church.

Day Ten

WHAT TO PRAY: For God's Spirit on Our Missionaries

Ye shall receive power, after that the Holy Ghost is come upon you: and ye shall be witnesses unto me. . .unto the uttermost part of the earth.
Acts 1:8

What the world needs today is, not only more missionaries, but the outpouring of God's Spirit on everyone whom He has sent out to work for Him in the foreign field.

God always gives his servants power equal to the work He asks of them. Think of the greatness and difficulty of this work—casting out Satan out of his strongholds—and pray that everyone who takes part in it may receive and do all his work in the power of the Holy Ghost. Think of the difficulties of your missionaries, and pray for them.

HOW TO PRAY: Trusting God's Faithfulness

He is faithful that promised. . . .
She judged him faithful who had promised.
Hebrews 10:23; 11:11

Just think of God's promises to His Son, concerning His kingdom; to the church, concerning the heathen; to His servants, concerning their work; to yourself, concerning your prayer; and pray in the assurance that He is faithful and only waits for prayer and faith to fulfil them. "Faithful is he that calleth you" (to pray), "who also will do it" (what He has promised) (1Thess. 5:24).

Take up individual missionaries, make yourself one with them, and pray 'til you know that you are heard. Oh, begin to live for Christ's kingdom as the one thing worth living for!

Day Eleven

WHAT TO PRAY: For More Laborers

Pray ye therefore the Lord of the harvest,
that he will send forth labourers into his harvest.
Matthew 9:38

What a remarkable call of the Lord Jesus for help from His disciples in getting the need supplied. What an honor put upon prayer. What a proof that God wants prayer and will hear it.

Pray for laborers, for all students in theological seminaries, training homes, Bible institutes, that they may not go unless He fits them and sends them forth; that our churches may train their students to seek for the sending forth of the Holy Spirit; that all believers may hold themselves ready to be sent forth, or to pray for those who can go.

HOW TO PRAY: In Faith, Nothing Doubting

Jesus answering saith unto them, Have faith in God. . . .
Whosoever shall say unto this mountain, Be thou removed,
and be thou cast into the sea; and shall not doubt in his heart,
but shall believe that. . .which he saith shall come to pass; he shall have [it].
Mark 11:22–23

Have faith in God! Ask Him to make Himself known to you as the faithful, mighty God, who worketh all in all; and you will be encouraged to believe that He can give suitable and sufficient laborers, however impossible this appears. But, remember, in answer to prayer and faith.

Apply this to every opening where a good worker is needed. The work is God's. He can give the right workman. But He must be asked and waited on.

Day Twelve

WHAT TO PRAY: For the Spirit to Convince the World of Sin

I will send [the Comforter] unto you. And when he is come,
he will reprove the world of sin.
John 16:7–8

God's one desire, the one object of Christ's being manifested, is to take away sin. The first work of the Spirit on the world is conviction of sin. Without that, no deep or abiding revival, no powerful conversion. Pray for it, that the gospel may be preached in such power of the Spirit, that men may see that they have rejected and crucified Christ and cry out, What shall we do?

Pray most earnestly for a mighty power of conviction of sin wherever the gospel is preached.

HOW TO PRAY: Stir up Yourself to Take Hold of God's Strength

Let him take hold of my strength, that he may make peace with me.
Isaiah 27:5

There is none that calleth upon thy name,
that stirreth up himself to take hold of thee.
Isaiah 64:7

Stir up the gift of God, which is in thee.
2 Timothy 1:6

First, take hold of God's strength. God is a Spirit. I cannot take hold of Him and hold Him fast, but by the Spirit. Take hold of God's strength, and hold on 'til it has done for you what He has promised. Pray for the power of the Spirit to convict of sin.

Second, stir up yourself, the power that is in you by the Holy Spirit, to take hold. Give your whole heart and will to it, and say, I will not let Thee go except Thou bless me.

Day Thirteen

WHAT TO PRAY: For the Spirit of Burning

And it shall come to pass, that he that is left in Zion. . .shall be called holy, . . .when the Lord shall have washed away the filth of the daughters of Zion, . . .by the spirit of judgment, and by the spirit of burning.
Isaiah 4:3–4

A washing by fire! a cleansing by judgment! He that has passed through this shall be called holy. The power of blessing for the world, the power of work and intercession that will avail, depends upon the spiritual state of the church; and that can only rise higher as sin is discovered and put away. Judgment must begin at the house of God. There must be conviction of sin for sanctification. Beseech God to give His Spirit as a spirit of judgment and a spirit of burning—to discover and burn out sin in His people.

HOW TO PRAY: In the Name of Christ

Whatsoever ye shall ask in my name, that will I do. . . .
If ye shall ask any thing in my name, I will do it.
John 14:13–14

Ask in the name of your redeemer God, who sits upon the throne. Ask what He has promised, what He gave His blood for, that sin may be put away from among His people. Ask—the prayer is after His own heart—for the spirit of deep conviction of sin to come among His people. Ask for the spirit of burning. Ask in the faith of His name—the faith of what He wills, of what He can do—and look for the answer. Pray that the church may be blessed, to be made a blessing in the world.

Day Fourteen

WHAT TO PRAY: For the Church of the Future

[That the children] might not be as their fathers, . . .a generation that set not their heart aright, and whose spirit was not stedfast with God.
Psalm 78:8

I will pour my spirit upon thy seed,
and my blessing upon thine offspring.
Isaiah 44:3

Pray for the rising generation who are to come after us. Think of the young men and young women and children of this age, and pray for all the agencies at work among them; that in associations and societies and unions, in homes and schools, Christ may be honored, and the Holy Spirit get possession of them. Pray for the young of your own neighborhood.

HOW TO PRAY: With the Whole Heart

The Lord. . .grant thee according to thine own heart.
Psalm 20:1, 4

Thou hast given him his heart's desire.
Psalm 21:2

I cried with my whole heart; hear me, O Lord.
Psalm 119:145

God lives and listens to every petition with His whole heart. Each time we pray, the whole infinite God is there to hear. He asks that in each prayer the whole man shall be there, too; that we shall cry with our whole heart. Christ gave Himself to God for men; and so He takes up every need into His intercession. If once we seek God with our whole heart, the whole heart will be in every prayer with which we come to this God. Pray with your whole heart for the young.

Day Fifteen

WHAT TO PRAY: For Schools and Colleges

As for me, this is my covenant with them, saith the LORD; My spirit that is upon thee, and my words which I have put in thy mouth, shall not depart out of thy mouth, nor out of the mouth of thy seed, nor out of the mouth of thy seed's seed, saith the LORD, from henceforth and for ever.

Isaiah 59:21

The future of the church and the world depends, to an extent we little conceive, on the education of the day. The church may be seeking to evangelize the heathen and be giving up her own children to secular and materialistic influences. Pray for schools and colleges, and that the church may realize and fulfil its momentous duty of caring for its children. Pray for godly teachers.

HOW TO PRAY: Not Limiting God

They. . .limited the Holy One of Israel.

Psalm 78:41

He did not many mighty works there because of their unbelief.

Matthew 13:58

Is any thing too hard for the LORD?

Genesis 18:14

Ah, Lord GOD! behold, thou hast made the heaven and the earth by thy great power. . .there is nothing too hard for thee. . . . Behold, I am the LORD. . .is there any thing too hard for me?

Jeremiah 32:17, 27

Beware, in your prayer, above everything, of limiting God, not only by unbelief, but by fancying that you know what He can do. Expect unexpected things above all that we ask or think. Each time you intercede, be quiet first and worship God in His glory. Think of what He can do, of how He delights to hear Christ, of your place in Christ; and expect great things.

Day Sixteen

WHAT TO PRAY: For the Power of the Holy Spirit in Our Sabbath Schools

Thus saith the Lord, Even the captives of the mighty shall be taken away, and the prey of the terrible shall be delivered: for I will contend with him that contendeth with thee, and I will save thy children.
Isaiah 49:25

Every part of the work of God's church is His work. He must do it. Prayer is the confession that He will, the surrender of ourselves into His hands to let Him work in us and through us. Pray for the hundreds of thousands of Sunday school teachers, that those who know God may be filled with His Spirit. Pray for your own Sunday school. Pray for the salvation of the children.

HOW TO PRAY: Boldly

We have a great high priest, . . . Jesus the Son of God. . . .
Let us therefore come boldly unto the throne of grace.
Hebrews 4:14, 16

These hints to help us in our work of intercession—what are they doing for us? Making us conscious of our feebleness in prayer? Thank God for this. It is the very first lesson we need on the way to pray the effectual prayer that availeth much. Let us persevere, taking each subject boldly to the throne of grace. As we pray we shall learn to pray and to believe and to expect with increasing boldness. Hold fast your assurance: It is at God's command you come as an intercessor. Christ will give you grace to pray aright.

Day Seventeen

WHAT TO PRAY: For Kings and Rulers

I exhort therefore, that, first of all, supplications, prayers, intercessions, giving of thanks, be made for all men; for kings, and for all that are in authority; that we may lead a quiet and peaceable life in all godliness and honesty.
1 Timothy 2:1–2

What a faith in the power of prayer! A few feeble and despised Christians are to influence the mighty Roman emperors and help in securing peace and quietness. Let us believe that prayer is a power that is taken up by God in His rule of the world. Let us pray for our country and its rulers; for all the rulers of the world; for rulers in cities or districts in which we are interested. When God's people unite in this, they may count upon their prayer effecting in the unseen world more than they know. Let faith hold this fast.

HOW TO PRAY: The Prayer before God as Incense

And another angel came and stood at the altar, having a golden censer; and there was given unto him much incense, that he should offer it with the prayers of all saints upon the golden altar which was before the throne. And the smoke of the incense, which came with the prayers of the saints, ascended up before God out of the angel's hand. And the angel took the censer, and filled it with fire of the altar, and cast it into the earth: and there were voices, and thunderings, and lightnings, and an earthquake.
Revelation 8:3–5

The same censer brings the prayer of the saints before God and casts fire upon the earth. The prayers that go up to heaven have their share in the history of this earth. Be sure that thy prayers enter God's presence.

Day Eighteen

WHAT TO PRAY: For Peace

I exhort therefore, that, first of all, supplications. . .be made. . .
for kings, and for all that are in authority; that we may lead
a quiet and peaceable life in all godliness and honesty.
For this is good and acceptable in the sight of God our Saviour.
1 Timothy 2:1–3

He maketh wars to cease unto the end of the earth.
Psalm 46:9

What a terrible sight!—the military armaments in which the nations find their pride. What a terrible thought!—the evil passions that may at any moment bring on war. And what a prospect the suffering and desolation that must come. God can, in answer to the prayer of His people, give peace. Let us pray for it and for the rule of righteousness on which alone it can be stablished.

HOW TO PRAY: With the Understanding

What is it then? I will pray with the spirit,
and I will pray with the understanding.
1 Corinthians 14:15

We need to pray with the spirit, as the vehicle of the intercession of God's Spirit, if we are to take hold of God in faith and power. We need to pray with the understanding, if we are really to enter deeply into the needs we bring before Him. Take time to apprehend intelligently, in each subject, the nature, the extent, the urgency of the request, the ground and way and certainty of God's promise as revealed in His Word. Let the mind affect the heart. Pray with the understanding and with the spirit.

Day Nineteen

WHAT TO PRAY: For the Holy Spirit on Christendom

Having a form of godliness, but denying the power thereof.
2 Timothy 3:5

Thou hast a name that thou livest, and art dead.
Revelation 3:1

There are five hundred millions of nominal Christians. The state of the majority is unspeakably awful. Formality, worldliness, ungodliness, rejection of Christ's service, ignorance, and indifference—to what an extent does all this prevail. We pray for the heathen—oh! do let us pray for those bearing Christ's name, many in worse than heathen darkness.

Does not one feel as if one ought to begin to give up his life and to cry day and night to God for souls? In answer to prayer, God gives the power of the Holy Ghost.

HOW TO PRAY: In Deep Stillness of Soul

My soul waiteth upon God: from him cometh my salvation.
Psalm 62:1

Prayer has its power in God alone. The nearer a man comes to God Himself, the deeper he enters into God's will; the more he takes hold of God, the more power in prayer.

God must reveal Himself. If it please Him to make Himself known, He can make the heart conscious of His presence. Our posture must be that of holy reverence, of quiet waiting and adoration.

As your month of intercession passes on, and you feel the greatness of your work, be still before God. Thus you will get power to pray.

Day Twenty

WHAT TO PRAY: For God's Spirit on the Heathen

Behold, these shall come from far. . .and these from the land of Sinim.
Isaiah 49:12

Princes shall come out of Egypt;
Ethiopia shall soon stretch out her hands unto God.
Psalm 68:31

I the Lord will hasten it in his time.
Isaiah 60:22

Pray for the heathen who are yet without the word. Think of China with her three hundred millions—a million a month dying without Christ. Think of dark Africa with its two hundred millions. Think of thirty millions a year going down into the thick darkness. If Christ gave His life for them, will you not do so? You can give yourself up to intercede for them. Just begin if you have never yet begun, with this simple monthly school of intercession. The ten minutes you give will make you feel this is not enough. God's Spirit will draw you on. Persevere, however feeble you are. Ask God to give you some country or tribe to pray for. Can anything be nobler than to do as Christ did? Give your life for the heathen.

HOW TO PRAY: With Confident Expectation of an Answer

Call unto me, and I will answer thee, and shew thee great
and mighty things, which thou knowest not.
Jeremiah 33:3

Thus saith the Lord God: I will yet for this be inquired of. . .to do it.
Ezekiel 36:37

Both texts refer to promises definitely made, but their fulfillment would depend upon prayer: God would be inquired of to do it.

Pray for God's fulfillment of His promises to His Son and His church, and expect the answer. Plead for the heathen: Plead God's promises.

Day Twenty-One

WHAT TO PRAY: For God's Spirit on the Jews

*I will pour upon the house of David,
and upon the inhabitants of Jerusalem, the spirit of grace and of supplications: and they shall look unto me whom they have pierced.*
Zechariah 12:10

*Brethren, my heart's desire and my prayer to God for Israel is,
that they might be saved.*
Romans 10:1

Pray for the Jews. Their return to the God of their fathers stands connected, in a way we cannot tell, with wonderful blessing to the church and with the coming of our Lord Jesus. Let us not think that God has foreordained all this and that we cannot hasten it. In a divine and mysterious way, God has connected His fulfillment of His promise with our prayer. His Spirit's intercession in us is God's forerunner of blessing. Pray for Israel and the work done among them. And pray, too: Amen. Even so, come. Lord Jesus!

HOW TO PRAY: With the Intercession of the Holy Spirit

We know not what we should pray for as we ought: but the Spirit itself maketh intercession for us with groanings which cannot be uttered.
Romans 8:26

In your ignorance and feebleness believe in the secret indwelling and intercession of the Holy Spirit within you. Yield yourself to His life and leading habitually. He will help your infirmities in prayer. Plead the promises of God even where you do not see how they are to be fulfilled. God knows the mind of the Spirit, because He maketh intercession for the saints according to the will of God. Pray with the simplicity of a little child; pray with the holy awe and reverence of one in whom God's Spirit dwells and prays.

Day Twenty-Two

WHAT TO PRAY: For All Who Are in Suffering

Remember them that are in bonds, as bound with them;
and them which suffer adversity, as being yourselves also in the body.
Hebrews 13:3

What a world of suffering we live in! How Jesus sacrificed all and identified Himself with it! Let us in our measure do so, too. The persecuted Stundists and Armenians and Jews, the famine-stricken millions of India, the hidden slavery of Africa, the poverty and wretchedness of our great cities—and so much more: What suffering among those who know God and who know Him not. And then in smaller circles, in ten thousand homes and hearts, what sorrow. In our own neighborhood, how many needing help or comfort. Let us have a heart for, let us think of the suffering. It will stir us to pray, to work, to hope, to love more. And in a way and time we know not, God will hear our prayer.

HOW TO PRAY: Praying Always, and Not Fainting

He spake a parable unto them to this end,
that men ought always to pray, and not to faint.
Luke 18:1

Do you not begin to feel prayer is really the help for this sinful world? What a need there is of unceasing prayer! The very greatness of the task makes us despair! What can our ten minutes of intercession avail! It is right we feel this: This is the way in which God is calling and preparing us to give our life to prayer. Give yourself wholly to God for men, and amid all your work your heart will be drawn out to men in love, and drawn up to God in dependence and expectation. To a heart thus led by the Holy Spirit, it is possible to pray always and not to faint.

Day Twenty-Three

WHAT TO PRAY: For the Holy Spirit in Your Own Work

I also labour, striving according to his working, which worketh in me mightily.
Colossians 1:29

You have your own special work; make it a work of intercession. Paul labored, striving according to the working of God in him. Remember, God is not only the Creator, but the great workman, who worketh all in all. You can only do your work in His strength, by Him working in you through the Spirit. Intercede much for those among whom you work, 'til God gives you life for them.

Let us all intercede, too, for each other, for every worker throughout God's church, however solitary or unknown.

HOW TO PRAY: In God's Very Presence

Draw nigh to God, and he will draw nigh to you.
James 4:8

The nearness of God gives rest and power in prayer. The nearness of God is given to him who makes it his first object. "Draw nigh to God"; seek the nearness to Him, and He will give it; "He will draw nigh to you." Then it becomes easy to pray in faith.

Remember that when first God takes you into the school of intercession it is almost more for your own sake than that of others. You have to be trained to love and wait and pray and believe. Only persevere. Learn to set yourself in His presence, to wait quietly for the assurance that He draws nigh. Enter His holy presence, tarry there, and spread your work before Him. Intercede for the souls you are working among. Get a blessing from God, His Spirit into your own heart, for them.

Day Twenty-Four

WHAT TO PRAY: For the Spirit on Your Own Congregation

Beginning at Jerusalem.
Luke 24:47

Each one of us is connected with some congregation or circle of believers, who are to us the part of Christ's body with which we come into most direct contact. They have a special claim on our intercession. Let it be a settled matter between God and you that you are to labor in prayer on its behalf. Pray for the minister and all leaders or workers in the church. Pray for the believers according to their needs. Pray for conversions. Pray for the power of the Spirit to manifest itself. Band yourself with others to join in secret in definite petitions. Let intercession be a definite work, carried on as systematically as preaching or Sunday school. And pray, expecting an answer.

HOW TO PRAY: Continually

Watchmen, . . .which shall never hold their peace day nor night.
Isaiah 62:6

His own elect, which cry day and night unto him.
Luke 18:7

Night and day praying exceedingly that we might. . .
perfect that which is lacking in your faith.
1 Thessalonians 3:10

A widow indeed, . . .trusteth in God,
and continueth in supplications and prayers night and day.
1 Timothy 5:5

When the glory of God and the love of Christ and the need of souls are revealed to us, the fire of this unceasing intercession will begin to burn in us for those who are near and those who are far off.

Day Twenty-Five

WHAT TO PRAY: For More Conversions

He is able also to save them to the uttermost. . .
seeing he ever liveth to make intercession.
Hebrews 7:25

We will give ourselves continually to prayer, and to the ministry
of the word. . . . And the word of God increased;
and the number of the disciples multiplied. . .greatly.
Acts 6:4, 7

Christ's power to save, and save completely, depends on His unceasing intercession. The apostles withdrawing themselves from other work to give themselves continually to prayer was followed by the number of the disciples multiplying exceedingly. As we, in one day, give ourselves to intercession, we shall have more and mightier conversions. Let us plead for this. Christ is exalted to give repentance. The church exists with the divine purpose and promise of having conversions. Let us not be ashamed to confess our sin and feebleness, and cry to God for more conversions in Christian and heathen lands, of those, too, whom you know and love. Plead for the salvation of sinners.

HOW TO PRAY: In Deep Humility

Truth, Lord: yet the dogs eat of the crumbs. . . .O woman,
great is thy faith: be it unto thee even as thou wilt.
Matthew 15:27–28

You feel unworthy and unable to pray aright. To accept this heartily, and to be content still to come and be blessed in your unworthiness, is true humility. It proves its integrity by not seeking for anything, but simply trusting His grace. And so it is the very strength of a great faith that gets a full answer. "Yet the dogs"—let that be your plea as you persevere for someone possibly possessed of the devil. Let not your littleness hinder you for a moment.

Day Twenty-Six

WHAT TO PRAY: For the Holy Spirit on Young Converts

Peter and John. . .prayed for them, that they might receive the Holy Ghost: (for as yet he was fallen upon none of them: only they were baptized in the name of the Lord Jesus.)
Acts 8:14–16

Now he which stablisheth us with you in Christ, and hath anointed us, is God; who hath also. . .given [us] the earnest of the Spirit in our hearts.
2 Corinthians 1:21–22

How many new converts who remain feeble; how many who fall into sin; how many who backslide entirely. If we pray for the church, its growth in holiness and devotion to God's service, pray specially for the young converts. How many stand alone, surrounded by temptation; how many have no teaching on the Spirit in them and the power of God to establish them; how many in heathen lands, surrounded by Satan's power. If you pray for the power of the Spirit in the church, pray specially that every young convert may know that he may claim and receive the fullness of the Spirit.

HOW TO PRAY: Without Ceasing

As for me, God forbid that I should sin against the Lord in ceasing to pray for you.
1 Samuel 12:23

It is sin against the Lord to cease praying for others. When once we begin to see how absolutely indispensable intercession is, just as much a duty as loving God or believing in Christ, and how we are called and bound to it as believers, we shall feel that to cease intercession is grievous sin. Let us ask for grace to take up our place as priests with joy, and give our life to bring down the blessing of heaven.

Day Twenty-Seven

WHAT TO PRAY: That God's People May Realize Their Calling

I will bless thee. . .and thou shalt be a blessing:
. . .in thee *shall* all families of the earth *be blessed.*
Genesis 12:2–3

God be merciful unto us, *and bless* us; *and*
cause his face to shine upon us. . . . *That thy way may be known*
upon earth, *thy saving health* among all nations.
Psalm 67:1–2

Abraham was only blessed that he might be a blessing to all the earth. Israel prays for blessing, that God may be known among all nations. Every believer, just as much as Abraham, is only blessed that he may carry God's blessing to the world.

Cry to God that His people may know this, that every believer is only to live for the interests of God and His kingdom. If this truth were preached and believed and practiced, what a revolution it would bring in our mission work. What a host of willing intercessors we should have. Plead with God to work it by the Holy Spirit.

HOW TO PRAY: As One Who Has Accepted for Himself What He Asks for Others

Peter said, . . .Such as I have give I thee. . . .
The Holy Ghost fell on them, as on us at the beginning. . . .
God gave them the like gift as he did unto us.
Acts 3:6; 11:15, 17

As you pray for this great blessing on God's people, the Holy Spirit taking entire possession of them for God's service, yield yourself to God and claim the gift anew in faith. Let each thought of feebleness or shortcoming only make you the more urgent in prayer for others; as the blessing comes to them, you too will be helped. With every prayer for conversions or mission work, pray that God's people may know how wholly they belong to Him.

Day Twenty-Eight

WHAT TO PRAY: That All God's People May Know the Holy Spirit

The Spirit of truth; whom the world. . .neither knoweth. . .
but ye know him; for he dwelleth with you, and shall be in you.
John 14:17

Know ye not that your body is the temple of the Holy Ghost?
1 Corinthians 6:19

The Holy Spirit is the power of God for the salvation of men. He only works as He dwells in the church. He is given to enable believers to live wholly as God would have them live, in the full experience and witness of Him who saves completely. Pray God that every one of His people may know the Holy Spirit! That He in all His fullness is given to them! That they cannot expect to live as their Father would have, without having Him in His fullness, without being filled with Him! Pray that all God's people, even away in churches gathered out of heathendom, may learn to say: I believe in the Holy Ghost.

HOW TO PRAY: Laboring Fervently in Prayer

Epaphras, who is one of you, a servant of Christ, saluteth you,
always labouring fervently for you in prayers,
that ye may stand perfect and complete in all the will of God.
Colossians 4:12

To a healthy man labor is a delight; in what interests him he labors fervently. The believer who is in full health, whose heart is filled with God's Spirit, labors fervently in prayer. For what? That his brethren may stand perfect and complete in all the will of God; that they may know what God wills for them, how He calls them to live, and be led and walk by the Holy Ghost. Labor fervently in prayer that all God's children may know this, as possible, as divinely sure.

Day Twenty-Nine

WHAT TO PRAY: For the Spirit of Intercession

I have chosen you, and ordained you, that ye should go and bring forth fruit . . .that whatsoever ye shall ask of the Father in my name, he may give it you.
John 15:16

Hitherto have ye asked nothing in my name. . . .
At that day ye shall ask in my name.
John 16:24, 26

Has not our school of intercession taught us how little we have prayed in the name of Jesus? He promised His disciples: In that day, when the Holy Spirit comes upon you, ye shall ask in My name. Are there not tens of thousands with us mourning the lack of the power of intercession? Let our intercession today be for them and all God's children, that Christ may teach us that the Holy Spirit is in us; and what it is to live in His fullness, and to yield ourselves to His intercession work within us. The church and the world need nothing so much as a mighty Spirit of intercession to bring down the power of God on earth. Pray for the descent from heaven of the Spirit of intercession for a great prayer revival.

HOW TO PRAY: Abiding in Christ

If ye abide in me, and my words abide in you,
ye shall ask what ye will, and it shall be done unto you.
John 15:7

Our acceptance with God, our access to Him, is all in Christ. As we consciously abide in Him we have the liberty, not a liberty to our old nature or our self-will, but the divine liberty from all self-will, to ask what we will, in the power of the new nature, and it shall be done. Let us keep this place, and believe even now that our intercession is heard, and that the Spirit of supplication will be given all around us.

Day Thirty

WHAT TO PRAY: For the Holy Spirit with the Word of God

Our gospel came not unto you in word only, but also in power, and in the Holy Ghost, and in much assurance.
1 Thessalonians 1:5

[Those who] preached the gospel unto you with the Holy Ghost sent down from heaven.
1 Peter 1:12

What numbers of Bibles are being circulated. What numbers of sermons on the Bible are being preached. What numbers of Bibles are being read in home and school. How little blessing when it comes "in word" only; what divine blessing and power when it comes "in the Holy Ghost," when it is preached "with the Holy Ghost sent forth from heaven." Pray for Bible circulation, and preaching and teaching and reading, that it may all be in the Holy Ghost, with much prayer. Pray for the power of the Spirit with the Word in your own neighborhood, wherever it is being read or heard. Let every mention of "The Word of God" waken intercession.

HOW TO PRAY: Watching and Praying

Continue in prayer, and
watch in the same with thanksgiving; withal praying also for us, that God would open unto us a door of utterance.
Colossians 4:2–3

Do you not see how all depends upon God and prayer? As long as He lives and loves and hears and works, as long as there are souls with hearts closed to the Word, as long as there is work to be done in carrying the Word—pray without ceasing. Continue steadfastly in prayer, watching therein with thanksgiving. These words are for every Christian.

Day Thirty-One

WHAT TO PRAY: For the Spirit of Christ in His People

I am the vine, ye are the branches.
John 15:5

That ye should do as I have done to you.
John 13:15

As branches we are to be so like the vine, so entirely identified with it, that all may see that we have the same nature and life and spirit. When we pray for the Spirit, let us not only think of a Spirit of power, but the very disposition and temper of Christ Jesus. Ask and expect nothing less: for yourself and all God's children, cry for it.

HOW TO PRAY: Striving in Prayer

That ye strive together with me in your prayers to God for me.
Romans 15:30

I would that ye knew what great conflict I have for you.
Colossians 2:1

All the powers of evil seek to hinder us in prayer. Prayer is conflict with opposing forces. It needs the whole heart and all our strength. May God give us grace to strive in prayer 'til we prevail.

Prayer Starters

TONI SORTOR
AND
PAMELA MCQUADE

Contents

Preface 55
Anger
Anger and God's Forgiveness 57
Coals of Fire 58
A Change of Heart 59
Kind Words to a Spouse 60
The Bereaved
The Depths of Grief 61
Jesus' Victory over Death 62
Filling the Emptiness 63
Standing Firm 64
Celebration
Rejoicing in the Lord 65
Believing Without Seeing 66
The Source of Joy 67
Joy in Uncertainty 68
Charity
Giving in Faith 69
Cheerful Givers 70
Blessings of Mercy 71
A Loan to God 72
The Church
Brotherly Love 73
Laborers with God 74
My Brothers and Sisters 75
God's Grace 76
Contentment
Waiting for the Reward 77
God's Blessings 78
A Broken Spirit 79
"Fret Not" 80
Correction
My Reactions 81
The Benefits of Correction 82

Adversity 83
A Father's Love 84
Courage
Hidden Strength 85
Strong Hearted 86
"Fear Not" 87
Love's Courage 88
Enemies
God's Protection 89
Service Without Fear .90
Warrior God 91
Peace 92
Faith
A Grain of Mustard Seed 93
Feeling a Bit Unsure .94
God's Rewards 95
The Gospel 96
Faithfulness, God's
My Rock 97
Impatience 98
His Steadfastness 99
My Unbelief 100
Fear
"Take My Hand" 101
Insomnia 102
Fear-Proof 103
Fear Versus Faith 104
Friends
When a Friend Marries 105
Friends, Not Servants 106
Faithful 107
Closer Than a Brother 108
Fruitfulness
In God's Season 109
The Fruitfulness of the Godly 110
Blessings 111
Old Age 112

Guilt
Self-Condemnation 113
Dealing with Guilt 114
God's Forgiveness 115
Guilt Free 116
Help in Troubles
God's Strength 117
Light in the Darkness 118
God, My Portion 119
My Stronghold 120
Holy Spirit
Groanings Which Cannot Be Uttered. 121
The Spirit of Adoption 122
A Gift 123
Walking in the Spirit 124
Hope
When Things Go Wrong 125
A Lively Hope 126
Hope in God 127
Salvation's Hope 128
Humility
Humility in the World 129
Twisted Priorities 130
Humble Prayer 131
Humility Versus Pride 132
Joy
Delight 133
The Joy of Salvation 134
God's Joy 135
My Strength 136
Loneliness
"Here I Am" 137
Not Forsaken 138
Comfort 139
Family 140
Longevity
My Times Are in Your Hands 141

"I Will Carry" 142
The Blessings of Long Life 143
God's Faithfulness 144
Love
Healing Love 145
Brotherly Love 146
Loving Righteousness 147
A Witness 148
Marriage
The Gift of Marriage 149
"I Am His" 150
Christ as Head 151
Married Honor 152
Meekness
"Nobodies" 153
Beautiful in God's Eyes 154
God's Judgment 155
Inheriting the Earth 156
Mercy
Hiding 157
Searching for Perfection 158
God's Mercy 159
Unearned Grace 160
Missionaries/Evangelists
A Prayer for Blessings 161
The Lord Enables 162
Good News 163
Preaching to the Nations 164
Money
Uncertain Riches 165
Taking Matters into My Own Hands. 166
Worldly Possessions 167
Peace 168
The Nation
Peace 169
Forest Fire 170

A Holy Nation 171
Prayer for the Nations 172
Obedience
Doers of the Law 173
Founded on a Rock 174
Prosperity 175
The World 176
Parenting
Correction 177
Sunflowers 178
Perfection 179
The Blessings of Children 180
Pastors/Leaders
Bright Spots of Light 181
The Fruitful Congregation 182
Leaders' Blessing 183
Teaching 184
Patience
Two Types of Patience 185
Waiting for the Promise .186
The Second Coming 187
Endurance 188
Poverty
A Prayer for Those in Need 189
God's Love for the Poor 190
The Poor and Evildoers .191
Spiritual Poverty 192
Prisoners
Prisons Without Bars 193
Judgment Is Yours 194
God's Power 195
God's Rescue 196
Repentance
God's Never-Failing Mercy 197
The Company of Sinners 198
Brokenhearted 199
Healing 200

Reproach
The Sting of Reproach 201
The Desolation of Reproach 202
God's Glory 203
Fear of Reproach 204
Righteousness
God's Provision 205
The Fruit of Righteousness 206
Glorifying God 207
When Doing Right Goes Wrong 208
Salvation
The Salvation of All 209
The Gift of Salvation 210
New Life 211
Seeking God 212
Sickness
A Prayer of Faith 213
A Prayer for Health Workers 214
Healed by Jesus 215
Protection 216
Sin
Avoiding Sin 217
God's Covenant 218
Repentance 219
Salvation 220
Success
My Thankfulness 221
My Blessings 222
My Stewardship 223
My Savior 224
Suffering
Consolation 225
Exceeding Joy 226
Comfort 227
Christian Suffering 228
Temptation
The Crown of Life 229

No Problem Too Small 230
God's Faithfulness 231
Jesus' Grace 232

Trust

Taking the Wrong Path 233
"Don't Be Afraid" 234
Worldly Cares 235
Mount Zion 236

The Unsaved

Waiting at the Door 237
Contact with the Unsaved 238
Enemies of God 239
Christian Fearlessness 240

Wisdom

Blessings of Wisdom 241
My Continual Source 242
Understanding 243
Walking in Wisdom 244

The Word of God

Becoming Wise 245
Eternal Life 246
Power 247
Spiritual Growth 248

The Workplace

Honest Work 249
Slack Hands 250
Flourishing 251
My Lifeline 252

The World

Lights in the Dark 253
God's Messenger 254
Safety 255
Separation 256

PREFACE

God's promises have richly blessed Christians through the ages. They have offered solutions to problems, strength during trials, and inspiration for the Christian life.

In these pages, we provide prayers based on many of Scripture's promises. Whether you are struggling with guilt or fear or need to draw close to God's loving heart, grab hold of a truth in Scripture and share a heartfelt prayer.

These prayers, designed for use in private devotions or small Christian gatherings, may be helpful for family prayers or small-group Bible studies. But most of all we hope they will draw you closer to God and inspire your own prayers. As you pray, you may wish to add your personal needs, those of your family and friends, or the concerns of your small group or congregation.

Pray, and experience the truth of God's promise to Jeremiah: "Call unto me, and I will answer thee, and shew thee great and mighty things, which thou knowest not" (Jeremiah 33:3).

1. Anger and God's Forgiveness

Let all bitterness, and wrath,
and anger, and clamour,
and evil speaking, be put away from you,
with all malice. And be ye kind one to another,
tenderhearted, forgiving one another,
even as God for Christ's sake hath forgiven you.
Ephesians 4:31–32

Father, You have taken my sins and put them far away from me, as if I had never sinned, for the sake of Jesus, my Redeemer. Yet still I fall victim to anger, wrath, and malice toward others, despite Your loving example. I live in a world full of anger, and I find forgiving difficult. In times of violent emotions, help me remember Your unending forgiveness and treat others with the kindness and compassion that You show to me every day of my life.

2. COALS OF FIRE

If thine enemy be hungry,
give him bread to eat;
and if he be thirsty, give him water to drink:
For thou shalt heap coals of fire upon his head,
and the LORD *shall reward thee.*

PROVERBS 25:21–22

Lord, my natural reaction to anger is to make life harder for my enemies, not easier. Not many people would offer to cook a steak dinner for a hungry burglar before sending him off with the silverware. Any enemy certainly would be taken aback by such a response. He might even feel guilty and ashamed.

You tell me I am to treat everyone—even those who hurt me—with love and concern, and You will reward me for my actions. The next time I am prepared to lash out at someone who has hurt me, let Your forgiveness and love be reflected in my response.

3. A Change of Heart

The Lord is gracious,
and full of compassion;
slow to anger, and of great mercy.
Psalm 145:8

O Lord, how I wish I, too, were slow to anger. I confess I'm too quick to say harsh words or hand out condemnation.

If You treated me the way I sometimes treat others, I would be in deep trouble. How glad I am that compassion and graciousness are the hallmarks of Your attitude toward me. Help me have that attitude toward others.

Lord, take this anger from me and make me more like You. Increase the flow of mercy in my life. I want to be just like You, Jesus.

4. Kind Words to a Spouse

A soft answer turneth away wrath:
but grievous words stir up anger.
Proverbs 15:1

Lord, give me kind words to say when I speak to my spouse. May my words be life giving, not a source of condemnation and anger. When I speak angrily, I can't expect my loved one to stay calm. I don't want to have an ever-escalating battle with my spouse.

Prosper my relationship by blessing it with truthful but gentle words that turn aside anger. I want Your peace in my marriage, not a constant barrage of hard words that spring from wrathful hearts.

Grant me Your peace through loving speech.

1. The Depths of Grief

For I am persuaded, that neither death,
nor life, nor angels, nor principalities,
nor powers, nor things present,
nor things to come, nor height,
nor depth, nor any other creature,
shall be able to separate us from
the love of God,
which is in Christ Jesus our Lord.
Romans 8:38–39

I am alone, Father, in the midst of a crowd of friends and relatives who have come to comfort me. I will not be consoled. I will not smile at the grandchildren; I will not joy in the sunshine. I feel only partially here because the one I love is dead.

I am loved. I know that. No matter how I feel or act, my friends and family love me. You love me. But for now, I will not be comforted. Perhaps tomorrow. I know You understand.

2. Jesus' Victory over Death

He will swallow up death in victory;
and the Lord GOD will wipe away tears
from off all faces.
ISAIAH 25:8

Father, right now, standing at the grave of one I love, I cannot be consoled by any words. I am capable only of weeping for my loss; all I can feel is despair and anger that my loved one has been ripped away from me. I am in shock, stumbling through my paces, letting others guide me during these horrible hours.

And yet this is a battle that is already won. Jesus, through His death and resurrection, has conquered death, "that whosoever believeth in him should not perish, but have eternal life" (John 3:15). I know this, Father. I believe this. Be with me today as I grieve. Wipe away my tears and give me faith in these dark hours, for the victory is already Yours.

3. Filling the Emptiness

I will never leave thee,
nor forsake thee.
Hebrews 13:5

How empty my life seems without my loved one, Lord. You brought us together for a time and filled our lives with good and bad times. I cherish the memories of both, but still these memories cause my heart pain.

Thank You for promising not to leave me, Jesus, even in this emptiness. When others disappear, You're right by me, no matter how I feel. I want to draw close to You today.

Fill my emptiness with Your healing love, Lord. Make me whole in You as You fill me with Your healing Spirit.

4. Standing Firm

The Lord also will be
a refuge for the oppressed,
a refuge in times of trouble.
Psalm 9:9

Painful changes have entered my life, O Lord. They put me on the defensive, and I've been fighting them until I'm weary and confused. Now I don't know where to turn.

As this grief attacks me, set me firmly in the refuge of Your Son, who never changes. Thank You that even when the enemy seems to overwhelm me, I have Jesus beside me. I can stand firm in oppression, knowing You are my refuge. I am running to You now, Lord, for that protection. Open Your fortress, and keep me safe in Your love, no matter what battles rage outside.

1. Rejoicing in the Lord

Light is sown for the righteous,
and gladness for the upright in heart.
Rejoice in the LORD, *ye righteous;*
and give thanks at the
remembrance of his holiness.
PSALM 97:11–12

Almighty Father of all creation, today I give thanks for Your bounty and rejoice in remembrance of Your holiness. This is a day of celebration and song, of joyfulness and sunshine—a day You have made for my enjoyment. Help me forget the cares of the world for today; fill my heart with light as Your blessings fall upon me, and I grow closer to You.

2. Believing Without Seeing

Whom having not seen, ye love;
in whom, though now ye see him not,
yet believing, ye rejoice with
joy unspeakable and full of glory:
Receiving the end of your faith,
even the salvation of your souls.
1 Peter 1:8–9

I am one of Your peculiar people, Lord, set apart from the world by both my beliefs and my actions. I have never seen even Your sandal prints at the edge of the lake, yet I follow You with all my heart. My ears have never heard Your voice, but I live by Your words. My fingertips have never brushed the edge of Your garment, yet I am healed. My belief is not based in my senses or my intellect but in Your never failing love, which saved my soul and promises me unspeakable joy.

3. The Source of Joy

I will praise the Lord
according to his righteousness:
and will sing praise to the name
of the Lord most high.
Psalm 7:17

Without You, Lord Jesus, my life would be weighed down by sin, so I begin my celebration by praising Your righteousness. You are my righteous, glorious Lord, the only One who heals my sin. I know my joy today comes from Your hand, and I thank You for it.

I especially appreciate Your blessings that have brought me here. Thank You for them. May my words today show that I recognize You as the source of all good things. I appreciate Your mercy toward me.

Thank You, Lord, for sharing my joy as well as my sorrow. Be with me in every moment of this celebration.

4. Joy in Uncertainty

Thou hast put gladness in my heart,
more than in the time that their corn
and their wine increased.
Psalm 4:7

Thank You, Lord, for allowing me to celebrate, even when life is uncertain. When I trust in Your salvation, I don't have to depend on circumstances for joy. As I follow Your way and receive the blessings of Your righteousness, my heart fills with joy.

Though I may not know the outcome of everything in my life, I am trusting in You, and I know You care for all my needs. How my heart rejoices that I can trust in You!

Thank You that I can celebrate Your love and holiness each day. May that celebration be sweeter because I have put my trust in You.

1. Giving in Faith

But when thou makest a feast,
call the poor, the maimed, the lame, the blind:
And thou shalt be blessed;
for they cannot recompense thee:
for thou shalt be recompensed at
the resurrection of the just.
Luke 14:13–14

Father, sometimes charity seems to be a thankless task. No one will ever repay me, and I see no immediate results to give me some sense of satisfaction. It's like dropping a penny into a bottomless well: I can't even hear it clink at the end of its fall.

Remind me that though the little I can give seems useless, when added to the little that millions give, my charity can make a difference. You recall every penny I drop into the alms box; the consequences of my charity are in Your hands. Help me to give in faith.

2. Cheerful Givers

Every man according as he
purposeth in his heart, so let him give;
not grudgingly, or of necessity:
for God loveth a cheerful giver.
2 Corinthians 9:7

Father, every evening between six and nine, they perch on the phone lines like birds of prey:

"How much can you pledge?"

"Please support me."

"My cause needs your help."

They never call during a commercial, and they are often demanding or downright rude when I say I cannot give.

It's very hard to be a cheerful giver these days. Surely You know this. Guide me as I choose among many worthy causes; make me conscious of the blessings You have given me; help me to be a cheerful giver.

3. Blessings of Mercy

He that despiseth his neighbour sinneth:
but he that hath mercy on the poor,
happy is he.
Proverbs 14:21

Forgive me, Lord, for looking down on those who lack money, possessions, or knowledge of You. I'm sometimes tempted to think I'm better than they are, though Your Word clearly states that's not true.

Help me to heed Your warning and eagerly share what You've given me with those in need. Remind me that I count on Your mercy in my life as much as they count on it in theirs.

Even when sin filled every corner of my life, You did not despise me. Your mercy turned me into a new person. May I share that blessing with those whose spirits or pocketbooks are needy.

4. A Loan to God

He that hath pity upon the poor
lendeth unto the Lord;
and that which he hath given
will he pay him again.
Proverbs 19:17

Lord, You have given me an opportunity to give, but I'm wondering if I can afford to do it. You know my financial situation and the needs of the future better than I do, yet I struggle with this choice.

Thank You for making Your will clear by calling my heart to give and offering me this promise: If I loan money to You, I will never lose. I offer my finances and future to You, knowing You will provide for me.

1. Brotherly Love

But as touching brotherly love
ye need not that I write unto you:
for ye yourselves are taught of God
to love one another.
1 Thessalonians 4:9

Lord, You have brought us together, sons and daughters all, and made us into one family, teaching every one of us to love our brothers and sisters in Christ. We are Your Church. We are different in many ways: rich and poor, black and white, male and female. Some of us lead and some follow, each according to the talents You have given us and the needs of the community. In many ways we are more different than we are alike, yet Your love for us knows no human boundaries. We are family. We are Your Church.

2. Laborers with God

For we are labourers together with God:
ye are God's husbandry,
ye are God's building.
1 Corinthians 3:9

Whatever we accomplish as a church we accomplish through Your help, Lord. The work is too much for me on my own; the world's needs are far too great for me to even make a good start. I would give up, but You urge me on. You take the little that I can do and magnify it into something wondrous. Through Your blessings, together we become blessings for others, one faltering step at a time.

Whenever I am tempted to throw up my hands in defeat, remind me that You are always with me, holding me up until the work is done. I am part of Your Body, and together we plant the seeds; You will send the rain and ensure the harvest.

3. My Brothers and Sisters

He that loveth his brother
abideth in the light,
and there is none occasion
of stumbling in him.
1 John 2:10

Lord Jesus, help me to love my brothers and sisters despite the distractions and troubles the world heaps on me. The things of this world will destroy my communion with You, if I let them. Keep me mindful that dissention with others also means I'm at war with You.

Instead of focusing on differences of opinions, help me to look at You, my perfect Brother. Then the small things will not make me stumble, and the large issues will be settled.

4. God's Grace

Grace be with all them that
love our Lord Jesus Christ in sincerity.
Amen.
Ephesians 6:24

I pray that Your grace will be with all those in my church, Lord Jesus. I especially lift up the church leaders and teachers, but may each person in the congregation feel Your wonder and outpoured love. Bless each one with a closer relationship to You.

I have received much of Your unmerited favor. Let that flow over in my life into my church and from there into the world. May my church be graced with a special sincerity that shows the world Your love. May Your grace shine out to all who meet us.

1. Waiting for the Reward

Let not thine heart envy sinners:
but be thou in the fear of the Lord
all the day long.
For surely there is an end;
and thine expectation shall not be cut off.
Proverbs 23:17–18

Sometimes I wonder, Lord: Why do sinners seem to flourish while Your people struggle to support their families? Is it better for me to be poor? Surely there are those better off than I who are righteous; couldn't I be one of them? I get tired and discouraged.

But You promise that all bad things come to an end; my heart's desire will one day be mine. Until then, give me contentment with the blessings I have and faith in tomorrow.

2. God's Blessings

But godliness with contentment is great gain.
For we brought nothing into this world,
and it is certain we can carry nothing out.
And having food and raiment
let us be therewith content.

1 Timothy 6:6–8

I have much to be thankful for, Lord. You have given me a family that loves me, a job that puts food on my table, a place to sleep in safety, and clothing to keep me warm. I have the necessities of this life and Your promise of the life to come.

Forgive me when I ache for a little more, especially for my spouse and children. I know You want the best for me, and You will provide it. My job is to live my life in a way that glorifies You. Everything beyond that is a blessing. I choose to be content.

3. A Broken Spirit

A merry heart doeth good
like a medicine:
but a broken spirit
drieth the bones.
Proverbs 17:22

If a broken spirit dries the bones, Lord, about now mine should be dust. I'm not at all content with my situation, and my heart is down in the dumps. Turn my spirit toward You again, where I can find the joy and contentment I'm missing. May I feel Your Spirit touch my heart, so that I may bring good to those I see each day. Help me rejoice in You, no matter what is going on in my life. I don't want sin to turn me into a pile of dry bones, and I don't want to share that attitude with others.

Pour Your blessed balm on my aching heart, O Lord.

4. "Fret Not"

Fret not thyself because of evildoers,
neither be thou envious against
the workers of iniquity.
For they shall soon be cut down
like the grass,
and wither as the green herb.
Psalm 37:1–2

Thank You for Your promise, Lord, that tells me that even the most wicked people cannot take the world out of Your hands. Before cold spiritual weather withers their hearts, may I reach out to evildoers with Your good news. Let none be cut down or wither because I would not share the contentment I find in You.

1. My Reactions

If ye endure chastening,
God dealeth with you as with sons;
for what son is he whom
the father chasteneth not?
Hebrews 12:7

You are my perfect Father, but I am Your imperfect child, full of human failings and sometimes in need of correction. If You did not love me, You would ignore my misdeeds, leaving me to my own devices and letting the chips fall where they may, but You do not do this. You love me and therefore correct me, as I do with my own children.

Like my children, I do not always welcome correction. I pout; I avoid You; I try to go my own way. I even say, "It's not my fault!" as if I were not responsible for my own actions. In times like these, be patient with me, Father, because I cannot live without Your love.

2. The Benefits of Correction

Now no chastening for the present seemeth to be joyous, but grievous: nevertheless afterward it yieldeth the peaceable fruit of righteousness unto them which are exercised thereby.

Hebrews 12:11

I try to mold my children, little by little, into people who follow You. I do this slowly and patiently, always with love, praying that my efforts will not be in vain.

Meanwhile, You have a vision of how I should turn out, too. Forgive me when I take Your correction poorly, Father. Often I cannot see the reasons for it and feel it is more of a burden than a blessing—but You never give up on me, no matter how stubborn I am. You teach and correct with love, and little by little I become the person You want me to be.

3. Adversity

Blessed is the man whom thou chastenest,
O Lord, and teachest him out of thy law;
that thou mayest give him rest
from the days of adversity,
until the pit be digged for the wicked.
Psalm 94:12–13

Like just about everyone, Lord, I don't enjoy being corrected. It seems more like adversity than love when You show me I've been wrong. Help me to see that only Your love prompts You to ask me to change. I can only have the good things You want for me by learning Your ways. Sometimes adversity is the only way You can teach me the lesson I need to learn.

Help me to walk more perfectly in Your path, so that I can find rest from adversity. Teach me Your way.

4. A Father's Love

For whom the LORD *loveth he correcteth;*
even as a father the son
in whom he delighteth.
PROVERBS 3:12

Only a parent bothers to lovingly tell a child that he or she has done wrong. Most people don't know the youngster well enough or care deeply enough to take the risk that comes with correction.

Thank You, Father God, for caring enough about me to tell me when I'm headed in the wrong direction. Even when I've gotten into a real mess and ignored Your warnings, You still pull me up, take me back to the place where I went wrong, and start me on a new path.

I appreciate Your love, even when the correction is painful. Thank You for being a loving Father to me.

1. Hidden Strength

He giveth power to the faint;
and to them that have no might
he increaseth strength.
Isaiah 40:29

I am not courageous, Lord. Like a child, sometimes I still wonder about the monsters under the bed and turn on every light in the house as soon as the sun sets. When I look at my life's challenges, I feel so small and inadequate.

Yet You promise courage and strength when I need them. Sometimes, in Your power, I even do remarkable things that cannot be explained; I can rise to great heights when necessary. After the danger is passed, my knees may give out, and I wonder how I did such wonders. Then the light dawns: You did wonders through me. Thank You for the hidden strength You give me—Your strength.

2. Strong-Hearted

Wait on the Lord:
be of good courage,
and he shall strengthen thine heart:
wait, I say, on the Lord.
Psalm 27:14

I'm scared, Lord. Please help me. I just don't think I can meet tomorrow's challenge.

In my own power, I know I'm too weak. But I have faith You will enable me to meet whatever challenges life brings. I'll wait for You, Lord, to empower me with Your Spirit. Strengthen my heart, Lord.

3. "Fear Not"

Be strong and of a good courage,
fear not, nor be afraid of them:
for the LORD *thy God,*
he it is that doth go with thee:
he will not fail thee, nor forsake thee.
DEUTERONOMY 31:6

I may not be setting out for the Promised Land, Lord, but I still have fears and doubts. Sometimes I face people or situations that seem to overwhelm me.

Like Israel, I can grip the promise that You will always be with me. Even when I face dark situations, I trust that You still walk by my side.

Today I need courage to step forward. Lift my heart with trust in You. Thank You that You never fail me.

4. Love's Courage

O love the Lord*, all ye his saints:*
for the Lord *preserveth the faithful,*
and plentifully rewardeth the proud doer.
Be of good courage,
and he shall strengthen your heart,
all ye that hope in the Lord*.*

Psalm 31:23–24

When my courage seems so small and slips away, when sin seeks to pull me from Your path, Lord, remind me of these verses. I need only trust in You, the One who keeps me safe and brings good things into my life. You reward my feeble efforts and multiply them through Your strength as I simply love You and respond to You in faith.

I want to be strong—in You and for You. Give me courage each day. When evil seems to abound and sin distracts me from Your way, thank You that Your love abounds still more.

1. God's Protection

Behold, all they that were incensed against
thee shall be ashamed and confounded:
they shall be as nothing;
and they that strive with thee shall perish.
Thou shalt seek them,
and shalt not find them.
Isaiah 41:11–12

Father, You have promised the righteous Your protection from their enemies. They may still come against me, but they will be powerless, ashamed, and confused by their inability to harm me. Your power against them is so fearsome that when I search for my enemies, I will not be able to find them.

Such protection is beyond my understanding but not to be taken lightly. You know exactly what I need when I call on You for help, and I trust Your decisions, especially when I am in fear for my life. Thank You, Father.

2. Service Without Fear

That he would grant unto us,
that we being delivered out of the hand of
our enemies might serve him without fear,
in holiness and righteousness before him,
all the days of our life.
Luke 1:74–75

Enemies come and go throughout my life. Some are serious dangers that require Your supernatural protection; others You allow me to handle with Your guidance. What have I done to deserve such protection?

I have tried to serve You, in some form or another, and You want me to be free to continue that service. You protect my back so my energy and actions are available for Your work.

Thank You for Your love and care, Lord. May my life reveal Your holiness and Your power, so others may come to worship You, too.

3. WARRIOR GOD

For the LORD your God is
he that goeth with you,
to fight for you against your enemies,
to save you.
DEUTERONOMY 20:4

Thank You, Lord, that You fight my battles for me. Just as when Israel went to war, I need You with me in physical battles and spiritual ones. Whether I need to recover from an illness or fight off sin, I cannot do it alone.

I rejoice that You are willing to take part in my battles and bring me out of them safely. No matter where I go, if I am doing Your will, I am safe in Your hand.

When my battles are successful, it is because You have gone with me. In my own strength, I have no power over my enemies; only Your hand can save me.

4. Peace

When a man's ways please the Lord,
he maketh even his enemies
to be at peace with him.
Proverbs 16:7

Lord, You know I want my ways to please You. Serving You is the greatest thing I can do with my life. As an added benefit, You have promised that because I obey, You will smooth my path. Even my enemies will become peaceful.

I've already seen Your promise at work in my life. Sometimes, when life seems to be getting rough, I pray—and the path becomes smooth before me. Issues I thought would become real problems turn into nothing at all, and I know You have answered my prayer.

Thank You for Your peace, which goes before me every day to bless my life.

1. A Grain of Mustard Seed

If ye have faith as a grain of mustard seed,
ye shall say unto this mountain,
Remove hence to yonder place;
and it shall remove;
and nothing shall be impossible unto you.
Matthew 17:20

A grain of mustard seed is so small it's nearly invisible. How could anyone who loves You not have at least that much faith? And yet even Your disciples failed from time to time because of unbelief.

This is a great mystery to me, Father. Some days my faith is so strong I can almost see it. I'm not quite up to moving mountains, but I feel Your power within me, and I dare to believe I am capable of anything. Other days, my faith seems puny and weak. Be with me on both my strong and weak days, because no matter how I feel, I want to do Your work.

2. Feeling a Bit Unsure

What things soever ye desire, when ye pray,
believe that ye receive them,
and ye shall have them.
Mark 11:24

Father, sometimes my prayers to You go unanswered or they're answered in such a way that I cannot recognize the answer. Sometimes the answers come years after the request; sometimes the answer is just "No." When that happens, I can only assume You have heard me and go on in faith.

Often, however, the problem is within me. My faith is shaky, and although I want my prayers answered, I doubt they will be. I am insecure about my worthiness, afraid I have asked for too much or offended You in some way, for I know how weak I can be. How foolish of me! I am Your beloved child, and You take great pleasure in giving me good things when I ask in faith. Make me bold; make me strong; help me believe.

3. God's Rewards

He that cometh to God
must believe that he is,
and that he is a rewarder of them
that diligently seek him.
Hebrews 11:6

Help me to diligently seek You, Lord. Whether or not I am seeing those rewards You promised, I know You provide good things for me. What I don't see today, You may provide another time.

Help me to seek You in faith for all my needs, mighty God. And let me reach out to those who do not yet believe in You. I need to share all You have done for me with people who have hurting hearts.

4. The Gospel

And he said unto them,
Go ye into all the world,
and preach the gospel to every creature.
He that believeth and
is baptized shall be saved;
but he that believeth not
shall be damned.
Mark 16:15–16

Faith in other things won't save me, Jesus. You commanded Your disciples to preach to the entire world, because only faith in You will bring anyone to faith.

I'm so glad that someone told me the good news that You came to save me. Thank You for that messenger who helped me understand my need. I want to pass on the same message to others who have never heard it. Open my lips and provide the words that will share Your truth with many.

1. My Rock

God is not a man, that he should lie;
neither the son of man, that he should repent:
hath he said, and shall he not do it?
or hath he spoken,
and shall he not make it good?
Numbers 23:19

Father, because I was made in Your image, I sometimes think I can project my own weaknesses back on You who have no weakness. I lie; I change my mind; I do not always honor my promises. All this is very human, but this is not a reflection of You. I make a grave mistake when I assume my faults are also Your faults.

You do not treat me as I treat others. What You promise, You will fulfill to the last word. What You say You will do, You will do. When the time comes for You to act, You will act. I may not always be faithful, but You always are. In a world where I am afraid to totally trust anyone, I know I can trust You. Thank You for being my Rock.

2. Impatience

Yea, I have spoken it,
I will also bring it to pass;
I have purposed it,
I will also do it.
Isaiah 46:11

Lord, forgive my impatience. I know You are faithful from generation to generation; I have no need to doubt that Your promises will be fulfilled. Yet I am like a little child on a long drive, asking, "Are we there yet?" anxious to be done with the tedious journey.

Unlike a vacation trip, my journey may go on for years. Some days I feel I will never get there, never see Your promises fulfilled. Even when one promise comes true and I reach one milestone on my path, I still worry about what's around the next bend. Some days I stamp my feet in impatience, while other days I fear the journey's end. Be patient with me, Father. This is all new territory for me.

3. His Steadfastness

Let us hold fast the profession of
our faith without wavering;
(for he is faithful that promised).
Hebrews 10:23

How could I trust You, Lord, if I had not seen how faithful You are to Your people? The testimony of the Old and New Testaments shows the world that You have never deserted those who believed in You. Because they experienced Your faithfulness, today people still follow You through the darkest situations, relying on Your promises.

Like Your long-ago followers, I want to cling to You. Let me not waver in my faith as I follow You. May my life become a testimony to Your faithfulness.

4. My Unbelief

If we believe not,
yet he abideth faithful:
he cannot deny himself.
2 Timothy 2:13

Thank You, Lord, that my faithfulness does not depend on my abilities. I try with all my might to be faithful, yet I can still end up in an awful mess. The good things I start often end up wrong. I hold fast to things I should let go and avoid things that would help Your kingdom grow.

I praise You for the faithfulness that is part of Your perfect nature. It never changes or leaves me helpless. Thank You for that faithfulness, Lord. May it seep into my heart and soul as I follow You today.

1. "Take My Hand"

For I the Lord *thy God*
will hold thy right hand,
saying unto thee,
Fear not; I will help thee.
Isaiah 41:13

Father, I taught my children not to step off the curb until one of their hands was firmly in mine. I guided them through crowds and past threatening dogs the same way. It's such an ingrained habit that sometimes I find myself reaching down to catch the hand of my grown (and mortified) children. I miss that little hand clutching mine in perfect trust. When old age catches up with me, the tables may be turned, and their hands may guide and support me.

Although I cannot physically touch Your hand in times of fear, I can feel Your presence, Your desire to protect and guide me as I once guided my children. I thank You for that, Father.

2. Insomnia

When thou liest down,
thou shalt not be afraid:
yea, thou shalt lie down,
and thy sleep shall be sweet.
Proverbs 3:24

I can't go to sleep, Father. I toss and turn while the fears of the day rampage through my mind:

"Why did I say that?"

"What should I have done instead?"

"Will I ever get a decent job?"

There seem to be a million fears, and tonight I know them all by name. If only I could fall asleep!

Then I decide to recall Bible verses, looking for ones that comfort and calm. I may stumble over the exact words, but I remember enough. Before I know it, I fall asleep—and my sleep is sweet. Thank You, Father!

3. Fear-Proof

And fear not them which kill the body,
but are not able to kill the soul.
Matthew 10:28

How wonderful, Father God, to know that even my most feared enemy does not have final control over me. Even if he put me to death, he could not part my soul from Your love.

I'm not facing death today, but I face fears that feel like death. That killjoy, Satan, tells me that by following You, I kill off every chance to fulfill certain hopes and dreams. A thousand small deaths attack my soul.

Keep me obedient to Your love; help me trust that You will bring me good things. I need faith to see blessings instead of fears.

4. Fear Versus Faith

And he said unto them,
Why are ye so fearful?
how is it that ye have no faith?
Mark 4:40

Lord Jesus, today I feel as if You are asleep while I'm all alone at the tiller of my life. Waves rise up around me, and You seem not to see them. The boat of my life rocks, and You don't grab the tiller from my hand. Fear fills my soul.

I know, Lord, that as a Christian I need not fear the waves. Doubt disrupted my vision and made me grab the tiller in the first place. Return my eyes to their proper focus: You.

1. When a Friend Marries

He that hath the bride is the bridegroom:
but the friend of the bridegroom,
which standeth and heareth him,
rejoiceth greatly because of
the bridegroom's voice.
John 3:29

My friends are marrying today, Lord, and their happiness makes me happy. I see in their eyes the awe and love they have for each other.

I can't help but be a little sad, because I know I am losing something here. We will always be friends, but from now on they will turn to each other first for help, advice, and fun. I understand this, though; that's the way You want a marriage to be. Bless these two friends of mine today. May they be as good friends to each other as they have been to me and others.

2. FRIENDS, NOT SERVANTS

Henceforth I call you not servants;
for the servant knoweth not what his lord doeth:
but I have called you friends;
for all things that I have heard of my Father
I have made known unto you.

JOHN 15:15

Lord, You kept no secrets from Your friends the disciples. Although they did not understand everything You told them or everything You did, You faithfully preached the Word of Your Father to each and every one of them, taking them into Your confidence.

You continue to offer me Your friendship today through Your Word and actions, forgiving my failings and weaknesses just as You did those of Your disciples. Like them, I often don't understand. But You will never give up on me.

3. FAITHFUL

A friend loveth at all times,
and a brother is born for adversity.
PROVERBS 17:17

Thank You, Lord God, for the faithful friends who have stood by me in adversity. Sometimes they seem more like brothers or sisters than my own siblings do. When that happens, my friends and I know it's because Your love fills our hearts. Thank You for giving me such relationships.

I, too, want to be a friend at all times, the way my friends have been to me. Help me choose my friends wisely and stand by them when they need encouragement or help. When life challenges their faith, I want to be standing right at their sides.

4. Closer Than a Brother

A man that hath friends
must shew himself friendly:
and there is a friend that
sticketh closer than a brother.
PROVERBS 18:24

Thank You, Jesus, for bringing me this friend. We've shared so much through Your love. Now help me follow Your example and stick closer than a brother to my friend in need.

Though Your touch may seem distant, help my friend cling to Your love. I trust that You will stick near us both as we walk together through this dark time.

Strengthen me to stay close to her during these struggles and show her Your love. By Your power, guide me to reach out. Use me to help meet my friend's needs.

Bless my friend, O Lord.

1. In God's Season

I am the vine, ye are the branches:
He that abideth in me, and I in him,
the same bringeth forth much fruit:
for without me ye can do nothing.
John 15:5

Father, sometimes I get ahead of You, so determined to bear fruit that it never dawns on me that fruit has its own season, and apple trees don't bear in February. Sometimes I'm just innocently eager; other times my pride is running the show. Either way, those apples will develop when You want them to, not when I say so, and I need to keep that in mind as I set out to accomplish Your work.

When some worthwhile project of mine fails for no obvious reason, remind me that I may be working out of season. I need to get in step with Your timetable.

2. The Fruitfulness of the Godly

And he shall be like a tree
planted by the rivers of water,
that bringeth forth his fruit in his season;
his leaf also shall not wither;
and whatsoever he doeth shall prosper.
Psalm 1:3

How nice it would be to be like that fruit tree, standing next to a river that never runs dry and keeps me green and healthy while my fruit matures. Conditions aren't quite that good these days. I'm surrounded by pavement and watered by runoff water. I wilt in summer and freeze in winter, so my fruit isn't exactly grade A.

Yet You promise me that if I am true to You, You will take care of me, and I will produce good fruit. What I cannot do on my own, You will accomplish, if I trust in You.

3. Blessings

For the Lord hath redeemed Jacob,
and ransomed him from the hand of
him that was stronger than he.
Therefore they shall. . .flow together
to the goodness of the Lord,
for wheat, and for wine, and for oil,
and for the young of the flock and of the herd:
and their soul shall be as a watered garden;
and they shall not sorrow any more at all.
Jeremiah 31:11–12

How many blessings You have heaped on me, Lord. Not only do You provide me with physical things; my spirit feels Your goodness. My soul flourishes, like a well-watered garden carefully tended by Your hand. You nourish my life and make it fruitful.

All my blessings flow out of Your salvation, Father. How can I thank You enough for Your love and care each day of my life? I can only offer my heart to You in obedience.

4. Old Age

They shall still bring forth fruit in old age;
they shall be fat and flourishing.
Psalm 92:14

No matter how old I live to be, You want me to bear fruit, Father God. Thank You for a promise that encourages me when aches and pains annoy me, and fears for the future fill my mind. When I live to serve You, through worship and obedience, I do not wither or faint.

Thank You for the fruit You have given me through the years: children, finances, and spiritual abundance, which have made me profitable for You. Let even my last years glorify Your faithfulness.

1. Self-Condemnation

For if our heart condemn us,
God is greater than our heart,
and knoweth all things.
1 John 3:20

I know who I am, merciful Father, and I find myself unworthy of You. Judge and jury would agree with my own self-condemnation. I sin, then I sin again; if You kept a list of my sins, it would be as long as Your mighty arm. Yet still I have hope for myself, because You forgive all my sins. Your unending compassion is beyond my understanding, but I trust in Your love each and every day.

2. Dealing with Guilt

I, even I, am he that blotteth out
thy transgressions for mine own sake,
and will not remember thy sins.
Isaiah 43:25

Sometimes, Father, I find myself striving for perfection, certain that I can live a holier life if I only work on myself a little more. Of course what happens is that I make progress on one particular sin at the expense of working on another and end up tormented by guilt.

Remind me that this is not a victory I can ever claim for myself. Sin is with me and will always be with me. Yet You promise that You will not even remember my sins because You choose not to! You sent Your Son to deal with my sin, and the job has been done. This is not a do-it-yourself project. Thank You, Father.

3. God's Forgiveness

For the Lord your God is
gracious and merciful,
and will not turn away
his face from you,
if ye return unto him.
2 Chronicles 30:9

How far I have strayed from Your commandments, Lord. It hurts to know how I've harmed You and those I love.

You've promised that if I return to You, You will not turn away. Forgive my sin, Lord, and help me make things right with those I've hurt. Help them to forgive my wrongs, too.

Turn my heart from evil, Jesus, and help me be more like You each day. Put this sin in my past—forever.

4. Guilt Free

As far as the east is from the west,
so far hath he removed our
transgressions from us.
Psalm 103:12

I can't seem to let go of some guilt, Lord. Thank You for reminding me that when You remove a wrong from my life, it's gone for good.

Help me to trust in Your words and put them to work in my life. When Satan reminds me of my past, let me drop the memory of that sin into the ocean of Your love.

Jesus, thank You for showing Your love for me by being the way to forgiveness. Without You there would be no distance at all between me and my sin.

1. God's Strength

The Lord *is my rock, and my fortress,*
and my deliverer; my God,
my strength, in whom I will trust;
my buckler, and the horn of my salvation,
and my high tower.
I will call upon the Lord*,*
who is worthy to be praised:
so shall I be saved from mine enemies.
Psalm 18:2–3

My Father, my strength, and my Redeemer, I cannot save myself from all that terrifies me. I cannot save those who love me and look to me for protection. The world presses in on me and defeats me, despite my best efforts, until finally I call on You for help and find You there, just waiting for me to ask. Great are Your powers, O Lord; great is Your mercy; great is Your love.

2. Light in the Darkness

Rejoice not against me, O mine enemy:
when I fall, I shall arise;
when I sit in darkness,
the Lord *shall be a light unto me.*
Micah 7:8

Troubles come from many sources: sometimes from enemies and sometimes from ourselves. I may stumble and fall because I was careless—or because someone gave me a good shove; it doesn't much matter how I ended up in this particular mess. When I fall, Your strong arm is there to help me up again. When I sit in darkness and turmoil, You will be my light.

You never promised my life would be easy, Father, but You do promise to be there for me in good times and bad, supporting me and leading me back into the light. You are my strength and power.

3. God, My Portion

My flesh and my heart faileth:
but God is the strength of my heart,
and my portion for ever.
Psalm 73:26

Without You, how could I face troubles, Lord? Alone, I'm so weak, prone to sin, and unsure of the solutions to my problems. But my spiritual and physical "failure" doesn't have to be permanent. You give me strength to continue when troubles assail me, by filling my heart with hope. As I trust in You, strength fills my entire being.

All that I am is tied up in You, Lord. Whether I face hard times or good ones, You are forever the focus of my heart.

4. My Stronghold

The LORD is good,
a strong hold in the day of trouble;
and he knoweth them
that trust in him.
NAHUM 1:7

Here I am, coming to You in trouble again, Lord God. Thank You for this promise that I can trust You to help me. I'm glad I can come to You, since no one else has a solution to my problem.

Thank You for being a stronghold, protecting me from harm. When I face troubles, I can count on the fact that they will only go so far. With Your strong hand, You hold back some of the enemy's attacks against me.

Help me continue to trust in You, Lord. I need to draw closer to You in faith.

1. Groanings Which Cannot Be Uttered

Likewise the Spirit also
helpeth our infirmities:
for we know not what
we should pray for as we ought:
but the Spirit itself maketh intercession for us
with groanings which cannot be uttered.
ROMANS 8:26

Some days it's hard to pray, Father. I need Your guidance because I hardly know where to begin, let alone what to say or how to say it. Even when I have no special needs or requests and just want to praise You for all my blessings, I have a hard time finding the "right" words.

When that happens, I am thankful for Your Holy Spirit, who knows exactly what I want to say and intercedes on my behalf when my tongue fails me. Thank You, Father.

2. The Spirit of Adoption

For ye have not received
the spirit of bondage again to fear;
but ye have received
the Spirit of adoption,
whereby we cry, Abba, Father.
Romans 8:15

Little children have many fears, some of which they cannot explain even to their parents. They run to their parents' room at night, cold and shaking in terror, and beg to be allowed into the big, safe bed. They know their parents will protect them from whatever fills their nightmares.

In the dark of the night I sometimes find myself in the clutch of fear, too. Because I am Your adopted child through Christ, I know You love me, and I cry out to You. Through Your Spirit, You calm and protect me as I cry, "Abba, Father."

3. A Gift

If ye then, being evil,
know how to give good gifts
unto your children:
how much more shall your
heavenly Father give the Holy Spirit
to them that ask him?
Luke 11:13

Thank You, Father, for Your wonderful gift of the Holy Spirit. What better present could enable me to live in a fashion that pleases You? When Your Spirit fills me with power, I can live for You.

Without Your gift, I would be empty, Lord. Thank You for not only saving me through Your Son, Jesus, but giving me Your power to make each day count for You. I need Your gift every day. Help me not to leave Your Spirit on the shelf but to make Him part of my life always.

4. Walking in the Spirit

And I will put my spirit within you,
and cause you to walk in my statutes,
and ye shall keep my judgments,
and do them.
Ezekiel 36:27

In my own power, Lord, I cannot walk in Your statutes. Even when my heart wants to obey, sin trips me. My heart and mind wander into places they have no business going. Instead of keeping Your judgments, I make my own weak ones.

Fill me with Your Spirit, so that I may glorify You in every choice I make. When my every thought and action are directed by Your Spirit, I cannot go astray. Give me the strength to obey You completely, so each second of my days may be filled with testimonies to You.

1. When Things Go Wrong

For thou art my hope,
O Lord God:
thou art my trust from my youth.
Psalm 71:5

Even as a child, Lord, I knew that things go wrong. Parents divorce, love is lost, pets die, and friends betray. As an adult, I know there are many things I cannot control, no matter how hard I may try, and many of life's events break my heart. But still I hope, because through it all I have You. You can heal even the deepest loss.

Thank You for this hope, for allowing me to lean on You in the bad times. With hope, anything is possible.

2. A Lively Hope

Blessed be the God and Father
of our Lord Jesus Christ,
which according to his abundant mercy
hath begotten us again unto
a lively hope by the resurrection of
Jesus Christ from the dead.
1 Peter 1:3

I know that hope comes in many forms, Father. There is grudging hope, reluctant hope, tentative hope, even doubtful hope. It is, after all, in my nature to hope, even when hope has failed me before and will surely do so again.

But You, through the resurrection of Your Son, Jesus Christ, offer me a "lively" hope, a hope that never disappoints or fails. When my human hopes turn to dust, Your promise abides: "For God so loved the world, that he gave his only begotten Son, that whosoever believeth in him should not perish, but have everlasting life" (John 3:16).

3. Hope in God

Believe in God,
that raised him up from the dead,
and gave him glory;
that your faith and hope might be in God.
1 Peter 1:21

My faith can't be in things or even other people. They fail me, Lord, as I quickly realize when I put my hope in anything that is not eternal. You alone are worthy to bear my hope. When I first gave my life to Jesus, I understood that I can trust You, not only for my eternal life, but also for every earthly thing.

Today I put my hope in You for the situations I am in, for the hurts that afflict me, and for each second of my future. I trust in You, Father, that You will raise me up, too, just as You did Jesus.

4. Salvation's Hope

For we are saved by hope:
but hope that is seen is not hope:
for what a man seeth,
why doth he yet hope for?
But if we hope for that we see not,
then do we with patience wait for it.
Romans 8:24–25

You have not only promised today's salvation, Lord, but an eternity of life with You. Today I see part of Your promise, in Your work in my life; but the greater part of salvation still lies ahead of me, a promise yet unfulfilled.

When doubts assail, increase my hope. Help me to wait patiently for that final salvation. My hope lies in You alone.

1. Humility in the World

And whosoever shall exalt himself
shall be abased;
and he that shall humble himself
shall be exalted.
Matthew 23:12

Father, humility is not considered much of an advantage in today's world. Instead I am expected to be self-confident and aggressive, to push my way ahead of others to get a better job, to be an instant expert, even if I have to fake it. I hear humility is for losers.

As a Christian, I know this type of life is not what You want for me. It's not what I want for myself, either. Whenever I feel pressure to exalt myself above others, remind me that my worth is found in You alone. Teach me to serve, to love, to be honest, to put the needs of others first; to live a humble but blessed life.

2. Twisted Priorities

By humility and the fear of the LORD
are riches, and honour, and life.
PROVERBS 22:4

Father, sometimes I get things backward, thinking that if I am successful in life I will be of better service to You. I'll have more money, more time. Then people will listen to me; I'll have influence and power to use for Your kingdom. Sometimes it does work out this way, but normally if I become successful, I end up doing no more work for You than I did before.

Help me to realize that humility and doing Your will should come first, no matter what my present situation is. Help me keep my eyes on You, and the rest will take care of itself.

3. Humble Prayer

When he maketh inquisition for blood,
he remembereth them:
he forgetteth not the cry of the humble.
Psalm 9:12

How many times, Lord, have I wondered if You heard my prayers? When wickedness surrounds me, and You don't seem to act, I blame the entire world or begin to think Your ears are closed.

If pride has caused my troubles, show me where it lies in me, Holy One. Humble my heart before You, so I can admit my guilt.

But if I must simply await Your moment for justice, let humility bring patient expectation that You will remember and act. You hear every breath of my cries when I obey You.

4. Humility Versus Pride

But he giveth more grace.
Wherefore he saith, God resisteth the proud,
but giveth grace unto the humble.
James 4:6

When the world makes pride look good, Lord, remind me that Your grace is for the humble. I turn aside from many "pleasures" in this world with a sigh, thinking I've lost out on something, but Your Word reminds me that those who resist You and Your will are the real losers.

Thank You for offering grace in increasing amounts. Encourage me in humility, that I may draw closer to You.

1. Delight

But let the righteous be glad;
let them rejoice before God:
yea, let them exceedingly rejoice.
Psalm 68:3

Heavenly Father, at times the joy seems to slip out of my worship. My singing becomes atonal mumbling; my prayers are dry words. I listen to the Word and preaching with one eye on my watch, and I leave the sanctuary with relief instead of joy.

You tell me to be glad, to rejoice before You, indeed, to exceedingly rejoice. Remind me of this when worship services become mere routine. Give the service leaders a new enthusiasm that catches my heart and brings it alive again, full of exceeding joy and delight at being Your child.

2. The Joy of Salvation

I will greatly rejoice in the LORD,
my soul shall be joyful in my God;
for he hath clothed me with the garments of salvation,
he hath covered me with the robe of righteousness,
as a bridegroom decketh himself with ornaments,
and as a bride adorneth herself with her jewels.
ISAIAH 61:10

I will never be rich, Lord. Every month I struggle to pay the bills, and there's little left for fun. My children will never go to a great university, and my retirement will not be a time of seeing the world.

Yet I am blessed with riches beyond counting. You have draped me in the garments of salvation and wrapped me snugly in the robe of righteousness. I am beautifully adorned by You—for You. You have given me all I need to live a joyful life, and I rejoice in Your gifts of beauty.

3. God's Joy

Yet I will rejoice in the LORD,
I will joy in the God of my salvation.
HABAKKUK 3:18

Even when life is miserable, I can rejoice in You, Lord. Pressures on the job and financial troubles can't stop that joy. Nothing disrupts Your plan of salvation for me or the change You've made in my heart.

Thank You, Lord, for lifting my heart in joy when I think of Your salvation. When the world seems empty or threatening, I can still rejoice. On even the worst day I can feel joy that You separated me from my sins and will never count them against me. Thank You, Lord.

4. My Strength

Then he said unto them, Go your way,
eat the fat, and drink the sweet,
and send portions unto them for whom nothing is prepared:
for this day is holy unto our Lord: neither be ye sorry;
for the joy of the LORD *is your strength.*
NEHEMIAH 8:10

Thank You, Lord God, for this time of rejoicing. Following times of trial, I've begun to see the good goal You had in mind all along. Thank You for guiding me on my way.

In these good times, I want to remember You and the strength You have given me. Because times are good for me, I should not begin to believe that I have achieved my success. When life seems flawless, I still rely on You. You remain my strength, despite my circumstances.

Let me use that strength to help others in need, so Your strength reaches the world.

1. "Here I Am"

Then shalt thou call,
and the LORD *shall answer;*
thou shalt cry, and he shall say,
Here I am.
ISAIAH 58:9

I'm lonely, Lord. I walk in the midst of a crowd and see no face I know; I hear a good story but have no one to tell it to. I sit in my pew at church, among others who share my faith, but none of them know my joys and fears. I know I am not alone in feeling this way, but that brings me no comfort.

Finally, in the dark of the night, I call out to You—and You are there. I tell You my problems, and You listen. I speak of the good things in my life, and You smile. I ask You for advice, knowing it will come in Your time. I am no longer lonely. I am loved.

2. Not Forsaken

But I am poor and needy;
yet the Lord thinketh upon me.
Psalm 40:17

Who am I, to come to You with prayers and thanksgiving, Lord? Who cares what I think? I am not a great person—not even a particularly good person. I will never do wonderful things or be loved by everyone who knows me. I will spend my life in loneliness and fear, just another nobody in a world full of nobodies.

But still You think about me. You don't just notice me and pass on—You actually take the time to think about me, to pay attention to me, to help me when I need help, and to protect me when I need protecting. I am not alone; I am not forsaken. Thank You, Lord!

3. Comfort

I will not leave you comfortless:
I will come to you.
John 14:18

A world without You, Lord, would be comfortless indeed. Now that You've entered my heart and filled me with Your love, I can hardly imagine not having the hope of Your love to guide me.

When I face trials that seem to separate me from You, I still trust that if I draw close to You, You will be my comfort. When life seems darkest, You will come to me, bringing Your peace.

No one can comfort like You, Lord. Reach into my soul today. I need Your Spirit's consolation.

4. Family

God setteth the solitary in families.
Psalm 68:6

However lonely I may become, Father, I thank You for my families—the one I was born into and the family of God, which supports me when my birth family is distant or unable to give me aid.

Thank You, Lord, that You care for my loneliness and give me a defense against it. Even when my own family fails to understand, You provide the arm of a brother Christian or the shoulder of my sister in Christ.

I'm so glad to be part of Your family, Lord. But most of all, I am proud to be Your child.

1. My Times Are in Your Hands

Thou shalt come to thy grave in a full age,
like as a shock of corn cometh in in his season.
Job 5:26

Father, I trust in the world to come but cling to the life I know and love today. Surely You understand the way I feel. Surely You wept when Your Son sacrificed His life at such a young age.

The time will come when I must say good-bye to those I love, when my body will be too sick and worn out to keep me here, when my season in this world will be over. I thank You for the many years You have given me and ask that You be with me and my family when my time does come. Comfort those I will leave behind, reminding them that I have had a full, productive life and that my time is in Your hand.

2. "I Will Carry"

And even to your old age I am he;
and even to hoar hairs will I carry you:
I have made, and I will bear;
even I will carry, and will deliver you.
Isaiah 46:4

Compassionate Father, Yours is the gift of long life, and I thank You for the bountiful years You have given me, years I never expected to see. Some people spend these extra years in good health until the end, but others bear the burden of poor health and failing finances. I do not know which to expect, but I know I don't want my children to have to carry me during these years; they have their own burdens and need no more.

Thank You for Your help, support, and provision as I age. May I use these years to glorify Your love, so that my life will serve as an example to younger generations of Your strength and care.

3. The Blessings of Long Life

With the ancient is wisdom;
and in length of days understanding.
With him is wisdom and strength,
he hath counsel and understanding.
Job 12:12–13

Father, through Your blessings our life span has become longer. In the past, our ancestors were fortunate to see their children reach maturity; most of them never saw their grandchildren. Now I will meet and enjoy my great-grandchildren. Not only is my life longer, so is my time of good health, the days I can fully enjoy.

Help me use this extra time profitably, I pray. A long lifetime of experience brings wisdom that should be shared. As I age, keep my heart young, my spirit strong, so I may do Your work throughout my life. I may be old, but I have much to contribute, with Your help.

4. God's Faithfulness

And thine age shall be
clearer than the noonday;
thou shalt shine forth,
thou shalt be as the morning.
Job 11:17

Thank You, Lord, for Your promise to make me shine, even in my last years. Physically I may not always feel perfect, but I can still glow for You with a peaceful and trusting spirit. Even when my body does not work perfectly, I can still pray for others. My work for Your kingdom may be just starting.

Keep me trusting in You, Father, aware that You have not left me by the side of the road. I want to reflect Your love and faithfulness every moment of my life.

1. Healing Love

I will heal their backsliding,
I will love them freely:
for mine anger is turned away from him.
Hosea 14:4

Even though I've slid away from faith, thank You, Lord, that I can hang on to this promise, which says You still love me. All I need to do is turn to You again for forgiveness.

Forgive me, Father, for my double-mindedness. Part of me wants to believe You, but fear and doubt have drawn me away from Your love. I don't want doubt to destroy my love for You. Heal me from the things that would separate us.

Yours is a wonderful love that does not count wrongs. Help me live in that love every day.

2. Brotherly Love

Beloved, let us love one another:
for love is of God;
and every one that loveth is born of God,
and knoweth God.
He that loveth not knoweth not God;
for God is love.
1 John 4:7–8

Thank You for the reminder that love is a three-way street, Lord. It doesn't simply depend on me and my brother or sister, but on You as well. Whatever my relationship, You have a part in it. I cannot fail to love a fellow Christian and not fail to love You.

You have promised that those who love are born of You. I don't want to act like someone who has never known Your love or healing power. Bring Your love into each relationship I have and let it be a testimony to Your ability to bring love into humble human lives. Fill my life with Your reaching-out love.

3. Loving Righteousness

The Lord openeth the eyes of the blind:
the Lord raiseth them that are bowed down:
the Lord loveth the righteous.
Psalm 146:8

Thank You, Lord God, for opening my eyes to see Your righteousness and raising me from my sin to new life in You. Without You, I would be blind and bowed down by sin. But Your love changed my life from the ground up.

On my own, I am never righteous. Certainly You could never love me for my deeds. Yet in Your generous, gracious love, You cared for me, even when I ignored You.

Help me to love others as You have loved me. I want to be part of Your mission to open blind eyes and raise bowed-down hearts.

4. A Witness

By this shall all men know that ye are my disciples,
if ye have love one to another.
John 13:35

Lord, I have to admit that loving my brothers and sisters in Christ can be hard. I tend to get caught up in what my "siblings" are doing and how I feel about it. Your promise that love will be a witness to the world sometimes seems impossible.

But how I feel about it doesn't change Your command to love. I know I can't love on my own; but through Your Spirit I can do all things—even this. When I seek to love others, I need to keep my eyes on You, not their flaws. Sweep away my critical attitude, and fill me with Your love.

1. The Gift of Marriage

Thy wife shall be as a fruitful vine by the sides of thine house: thy children like olive plants round about thy table.

Psalm 128:3

You have promised a good measure of happiness to those who love You, Father, and part of that happiness is the joy of a good marriage. Such a marriage is an unending feast; the fruits of fidelity and lifelong companionship are ours for the taking. Marriage is also a journey of discovery that never bores. There is always something new to discover about the one I love, new depths, new interests, new joys to be explored.

Thank You for the gift of love and marriage. May I handle it with care, for it is most precious.

2. "I Am His"

My beloved is mine, and I am his.
Song of Solomon 2:16

I am reluctant to say that any other person is mine or that I belong to someone else, Father. My independence is important in a world still afflicted with many types of slavery, and no matter how much I love another, I tend to hold some things back, just for myself.

But I do not come to the marriage altar in chains. I come willingly, even eagerly, bringing with me the most holy wedding gift of all—my total commitment to another person. Marriage makes us stronger; together we are more than we could ever be alone. Where once there were two, now there is one.

3. Christ as Head

For the husband is the head of the wife,
even as Christ is the head of the church:
and he is the saviour of the body.
Ephesians 5:23

O Lord, this verse makes me nervous. But thank You for the promise that Jesus is the head of the church. In You, I share a unity that goes beyond what this world offers. Your love brings spiritual unity, not just physical togetherness. You designed my marriage relationship to be a reflection of Your sacrificial love.

I don't want to argue over who is in charge in a marriage. That's not Your goal for my love. Instead, lead me into communion with You. May my unity with my spouse lead others to love You, too.

4. Married Honor

Likewise, ye husbands,
dwell with them according to knowledge,
giving honour unto the wife,
as unto the weaker vessel,
and as being heirs together of the grace of life;
that your prayers be not hindered.
1 Peter 3:7

What a wonderful relationship You've given us in marriage, Lord. This kind of sharing doesn't happen anyplace else. But I confess I don't always honor my spouse as I should. Sometimes I see her as someone who gets in my way, instead of a woman I need to treat gently.

When I forget to honor her, though, my relationship with You suffers. Keep me faithful to You in my marriage, so that both my relationship with You and the one with my wife will grow.

1. "Nobodies"

But let it be the hidden man of the heart,
in that which is not corruptible,
even the ornament of a meek and quiet spirit,
which is in the sight of God of great price.
1 Peter 3:4

Father, many in this world might consider themselves "nobodies"—the poor, the oppressed, the hardworking who have no special claim to fame or fortune. The meek and humble people who go quietly through their lives rarely consider themselves valuable to anyone.

But You tell me these people are made beautiful by their meek and quiet spirits; they are ornaments You value greatly, jewels of great price. Thank You for this hidden gift, Father. Thank You for telling me that even the smallest person is a source of joy for You.

2. Beautiful in God's Eyes

For the LORD *taketh pleasure in his people: he will beautify the meek with salvation.*
PSALM 149:4

Father, when I watch television, I begin to wonder what's wrong with me. There are no ugly people there; even the villains have perfect hair. Everyone is tall, few are weak or frightened, and none seem to worry about how to pay the rent or feed their families.

Remind me that television is fiction, Father, and that I do not have to be physically beautiful to be loved by You. You love the short, the impaired, those who struggle with life and sometimes go under. You love me so much that You call me forth by name and beautify me with Your salvation, the most precious ornament I could ever wish for.

3. God's Judgment

But with righteousness shall he judge the poor, and reprove with equity for the meek of the earth.

Isaiah 11:4

Forgive me, Lord, for the proud judgments I have made against those who don't own much in this world. I know You don't judge according to what a person owns or what's in a bank account, but sometimes I do. Thank You for this reminder of what's really important.

No matter how much I have in the bank or in my home, I, too, can be meek if You make me so. If I am humble toward You and others, You will not need to reprove me for my sins.

Thank You for Your justice to all—even to me, when I am poor in spirit or in worldly possessions.

4. Inheriting the Earth

But the meek shall inherit the earth;
and shall delight themselves in
the abundance of peace.
Psalm 37:11

Meekness doesn't seem the key to inheriting things in this world, Lord. When I allow others to "get ahead" of me, I usually end up losing money or power. How good it is to know that, in the end, inheriting the earth isn't a matter of pushing and shoving or making sure I get what's "due" me.

Even if I don't inherit much today, give me the abundant peace You promise—the peace of knowing that I've done Your will. Someday I know I'll have a "plot of land" in Your kingdom.

1. Hiding

And therefore will the Lord wait,
that he may be gracious unto you,
and therefore will he be exalted,
that he may have mercy upon you.
Isaiah 30:18

Sometimes I decide it would be safest to run and hide from You, Father, like a child hiding in a corner on a day he has done wrong. Maybe if I stay still You will forget about me. Maybe You will come looking for me and not see me. I have sinned, and I am afraid.

But You are not eager to punish me. You hold out Your hands to me, waiting patiently for me to return to You. How could I not return? You are my life and hope, so I come back to take my punishment, always surprised to find You offer mercy instead of anger and pain. Thank You, Father, for Your patience and love.

2. Searching for Perfection

Like as a father pitieth his children,
so the Lord pitieth them that fear him.
Psalm 103:13

Lord, I have sinned—again. Every day is a struggle, and I am rarely victorious. Some days I'm better than on other days, but I will never be perfect, and that depresses me.

Then my child comes to me, admitting to some wrong she has committed, some little childish thing that torments her but could hardly be helped, considering the circumstances. I hold her tightly and reassure her of my love. I tell her not to worry, that she is still a good girl. She doesn't have to be perfect to be loved.

Neither do I.

3. God's Mercy

And the sons of strangers
shall build up thy walls,
and their kings shall minister unto thee:
for in my wrath I smote thee,
but in my favour have I had mercy on thee.
Isaiah 60:10

Even in the midst of punishment for my sins, You have mercy on me, Lord. Though I could never do enough things right to earn such favor, You offer it freely.

When sin has made me lose control of my life, and I experience its pain, You do not leave me there. Suffering lasts for a while, but it is not Your final goal for me. Mercy is.

Pour forth Your mercy on my life and help me share it with others who need to depart from sin. May their hearts, too, turn to You.

4. Unearned Grace

And I will have mercy upon her
that had not obtained mercy;
and I will say to them
which were not my people,
Thou art my people;
and they shall say, Thou art my God.
Hosea 2:23

O Lord, how great is Your mercy to me. You owed me nothing, because I paid You no heed, yet You called me. When I walked far from You, You called me to turn to Your path.

Thank You for caring for me when I wallowed in sin. I did nothing to earn Your grace, yet You gave it to me anyway. May Your great mercy be reflected in my life as I pass on mercy to those who sin against me. May mercy flow freely in my life.

1. A Prayer for Blessings

Verily I say unto you,
There is no man that hath left house,
or parents, or brethren, or wife, or children,
for the kingdom of God's sake,
who shall not receive manifold
more in this present time,
and in the world to come life everlasting.
Luke 18:29–30

Father, I thank You for those who do the work of the missionary or evangelist, whether they work among us here at home or thousands of miles away in another land. They have given up so much to do Your will, and their rewards seem so few. I ask You to bless them and their efforts on behalf of the church, to show me their needs so I may support them, and to give them Your protection and guidance, wherever they may be. Keep them in my mind and heart, and bless their efforts for Your glory.

2. The Lord Enables

And I thank Christ Jesus our Lord,
who hath enabled me,
for that he counted me faithful,
putting me into the ministry.
1 Timothy 1:12

Lord, on my own, I am not capable of doing Your work as a preacher or evangelist. The life is hard, and I am weak. But You take me as I am and mold me into an individual capable of more than I ever imagined. Only You know my talents and abilities and call me to the type of service best suited for me. Forgive my doubts and fears and show me where I am needed, that Your will shall be done.

3. Good News

Therefore my people shall know my name:
therefore they shall know in that day
that I am he that doth speak:
behold, it is I.
How beautiful upon the mountains are
the feet of him that bringeth good tidings,
that publisheth peace.
Isaiah 52:6–7

How glad I am, Lord, that You sent me a messenger with the good news so that I could have peace with You. Whether it was a trained evangelist or a hometown missionary who spoke across the coffee cups, that person brought precious news.

Bless those who take Your Word to people who have never heard it. Whether Your messengers live in a foreign place or have an outreach within my own church, bless them and their message. May they publish peace to all the world.

4. Preaching to the Nations

And this gospel of the kingdom
shall be preached in all the world
for a witness unto all nations;
and then shall the end come.
Matthew 24:14

Thank You, Lord, that You cared not just about a few people, but that You sent the gospel message to the entire world. If You hadn't, I might never have heard Your truth or come to know You.

As missionaries seek to bring the gospel into the entire world, I ask Your blessing on them. May their witness be a bright one that clearly reflects Your love. Be with them in their trials and joys, and increase Your witness to every nation. May their testimony remain constantly faithful to You until the end comes.

1. Uncertain Riches

Charge them that are rich in this world,
that they be not highminded,
nor trust in uncertain riches,
but in the living God,
who giveth us richly all things to enjoy.
1 Timothy 6:17

Heavenly Father, compared to the rest of the world, I am rich and living a good life. My basic needs are being met, and I have an abundance of funds. Keep me mindful of my blessings, no matter how much or how little I have. Encourage me to use what I have in a way that brings glory to You. Riches can fade away in the blink of an eye; only You remain faithful forever.

2. Taking Matters into My Own Hands

A faithful man shall abound with blessings:
but he that maketh haste to be rich
shall not be innocent.
Proverbs 28:20

Father, You give richly to Your children. Everything I need to live a fulfilling life is mine for the asking, but blessings come in Your time, not mine. Sometimes I grow weary of waiting, thinking that if I could only have a little more money, I would be even happier. I give up on faithful waiting and take matters into my own hands. I work long hours, ignoring the needs of my family. I harden my heart and walk over others at work to get to the next level. I hide my wallet when those in need ask me for help.

Help me keep my priorities in order, Father, trusting that You will provide what I need, when I need it, how I need it.

3. Worldly Possessions

But thou shalt remember the LORD thy God:
for it is he that giveth thee
power to get wealth,
that he may establish his covenant
which he sware unto thy fathers,
as it is this day.

DEUTERONOMY 8:18

I don't think of what I have as wealth, Lord; it isn't enough to buy out a major corporation. But You've given me enough to fulfill Your covenant. You've cared for me every day of my life. I haven't appreciated enough how You've taken care of me or the way You have kept me going, even in rough times.

You've also given me countless spiritual blessings: a church to worship in, Christian friends, and Your love.

Thank You for the spiritual and financial wealth You've given me. I want to use it to Your glory. Show me how to spend it for You this day.

4. Peace

The sleep of a labouring man is sweet,
whether he eat little or much:
but the abundance of the rich
will not suffer him to sleep.
There is a sore evil which
I have seen under the sun, namely,
riches kept for the owners thereof to their hurt.
But those riches perish by evil travail:
and he begetteth a son,
and there is nothing in his hand.
ECCLESIASTES 5:12–14

If more money will make me miserable, Lord, I'd rather not have it. I'd prefer Your peace to anxiety.

You've told me money can make me self-centered and selfish, as I start focusing on how much I have. I don't want to be that sort of person. When You bless me with more, make me generous, too.

I need to trust in Your provision, Father. Be in charge of my wallet and the rest of my life.

1. Peace

And the work of righteousness shall be peace;
and the effect of righteousness
quietness and assurance for ever.
Isaiah 32:17

Father, today I ask for the blessing of peace upon my nation, that my sons and daughters never experience war in their lifetimes but grow old in quietness and assurance. I understand that in order for that to happen, we must seek righteousness, not only personally but in the actions of our country itself.

Give our leaders insight into the need for justice for all, wherever they may live or whatever they may believe. Teach us humility and responsibility, so Your world may be a safe home for every citizen of every country. We need Your peace to cover us all.

2. Forest Fire

Now the Lord of peace himself
give you peace always by all means.
2 Thessalonians 3:16

People seem incapable of living in peace, Father. Wars flare up in one location, die down, then appear elsewhere, like a forest fire that never dies. While no worldwide fire burns and destroys today, for which I thank You, this world's disturbances never seem to end.

But while we are incapable of assuring peace, You are capable. Open my mind and heart to Your will and guidance; help me live as a citizen of a righteous nation; put out the forest fire of war. Bring lasting peace and justice to the world You love so much.

3. A Holy Nation

Now therefore,
if ye will obey my voice indeed,
and keep my covenant,
then ye shall be a peculiar treasure
unto me above all people:
for all the earth is mine:
and ye shall be unto me
a kingdom of priests,
and an holy nation.
Exodus 19:5–6

Sometimes, Lord, I don't feel like a peculiar treasure, just peculiar, since standing up for You is rarely popular. Thank You for this promise that as I obey, You'll make me part of a kingdom of priests in a holy nation. This is a goal for me to aim toward when I stand up for Your will in this sinful world.

Your kingdom is better than this world could ever be. I want to be an active part of it now.

4. Prayer for the Nations

If my people, which are called by my name,
shall humble themselves,
and pray, and seek my face,
and turn from their wicked ways,
then will I hear from heaven,
and will forgive their sin,
and will heal their land.
2 Chronicles 7:14

How desperately our land needs Your healing, Lord. I see wickedness spreading across it, and I wonder how this happened. A solution seems so far away.

The solution You've outlined in this promise is not without personal cost. You call on me to humble myself, seek You in prayer, and turn from my wicked ways. Today I confess that I have many sins to my credit and not much good. I turn from sin. Please bring me forgiveness and healing.

May I be a part of my hurting country's healing, Lord. Turn our leaders and people toward You—perhaps by using our testimonies for You today.

1. Doers of the Law

For not the hearers of the law
are just before God,
but the doers of the law shall be justified.
Romans 2:13

Sometimes I hear Your law at church, Lord, nod my head in agreement, then go out and do nothing. Worship is over, and I feel good about my faith. I got what I came for; I am saved, and that's enough.

In my heart I know better. I am aware that my personal salvation comes at great cost to You; I must not wrap it up and hide it safely in a closet. Instead, I should wear it boldly across my shoulders for all to see. I should wrap it around someone suffering in the cold; I should use it to feed the hungry and demonstrate Your love to all. Make me a doer of the law, Father, not just a hearer.

2. Founded on a Rock

Therefore whosoever heareth
these sayings of mine, and doeth them,
I will liken him unto a wise man,
which built his house upon a rock:
And the rain descended,
and the floods came, and the winds blew,
and beat upon that house;
and it fell not:
for it was founded upon a rock.
Matthew 7:24–25

All of us build our lives on something or around something—money, family, truth, love, even fear. Most of the time my foundation is buried under the soil where it is not seen by others, but it is still there, grounding my life and actions. Often my foundation is undependable and can send my life tumbling down after one bad storm. Teach me to ground my life on You, Lord, the only Rock who will stand forever against any storm.

3. Prosperity

Keep therefore the words
of this covenant,
and do them,
that ye may prosper
in all that ye do.
DEUTERONOMY 29:9

It's almost scary, Lord, to think that obedience could bring such blessing. I have a hard time believing that You would bless everything I do, if I obey You. Maybe that's because obedience is so hard for me.

I know I can't obey all on my own, Lord. When I try harder, I just get tied up in all the good I want to do and the evil that still pops out of me. Obedience can even become a matter of trying to earn prosperity.

Make my heart all Yours, Lord, and I will no longer struggle with sin. When my soul prospers, surely my life will be blessed.

4. The World

And the world passeth away,
and the lust thereof:
but he that doeth the will of God
abideth for ever.
1 John 2:17

This world seems so permanent and unchanging, Lord. But You alone created it, and You alone outlast it. Turn me from the lusts that focus my eyes on the temporary and keep them from You. Today's temptations and trials will seem small in the light of eternity.

I'm prone to live only in the here and now, and but for Your calling, that's all I would ever know. Thank You for showing me Your unending kingdom and inviting me to share it with You. I want to spend eternity with You.

1. Correction

Correct thy son, and he shall give thee rest;
yea, he shall give delight unto thy soul.
Proverbs 29:17

Father of all, give me wisdom as I raise my children. I want them to grow into godly adults, people who care for others and follow the path that leads to You. Sometimes this is difficult, and correction may be needed, so I ask You to show me how best to guide them. Help me not to be harsh or in any way abusive, yet still be an effective teacher and a good example.

You have entrusted these children to my care, and I love them without reservation, just as You love me. May I serve as an example of Your patience and undying love when I must correct my children.

2. Sunflowers

The father of the righteous shall greatly rejoice:
and he that begetteth a wise child
shall have joy of him.
Proverbs 23:24

As my children mature and grow, I am constantly amazed by the wisdom they often show: their kindness, their responsibility, their abilities. They still have their rough spots, but watching them mature is like watching a sunflower grow to unexpected heights. I may have planted the seed and cared for the young plant, but who knew it would turn out so beautifully? This is more than I ever expected.

I realize, Lord, that You had more to do with the flowering of my children than I. I did the best I could, and You magnified my efforts. Thank You for all those years of effort You put into my children. May You rejoice in them as much as I do today.

3. Perfection

Fathers, provoke not
your children to anger,
lest they be discouraged.
Colossians 3:21

Lord, I know I am not a perfect parent or a perfect Christian, but I am an adult, used to my failings and the failings of others. My children, however, still believe in Superman. Anything seems possible to them, so when I set impossibly high standards for them and they fail, they don't just shrug off their mistakes. They become discouraged and angry. They want to give up.

Teach me not to expect perfection from mere children. Help me explain that I am far from perfect and I know they will make mistakes, too. Let me show them that I will always love them, as You love me. I don't want to ever be a source of discouragement to them.

4. The Blessings of Children

And let us not be weary in well doing:
for in due season we shall reap, if we faint not.
Galatians 6:9

Parenting is a long-term project that never really ends. It's an intensive, hands-on calling with ridiculous work hours and no time off for good behavior. If it paid by the hour, I'd need no retirement plan at all.

Parenting's rewards are not always what I expect. Often they are priceless. An older brother shelters his pesky sister from a bully, willing to take any blows directed at her. A grown man kneels in front of his grandfather's chair to help him open a present while they talk of days gone by. A daughter brings her widowed mother on a family vacation to enjoy the grandchildren's reaction to Disneyland.

Thank You, Father, for these children and all the blessings they have brought in the past and will continue to bring in the future.

1. Bright Spots of Light

How then shall they call on him
in whom they have not believed?
and how shall they believe in him
of whom they have not heard?
and how shall they hear without a preacher?
Romans 10:14

Father, I ask that You watch over my leaders today and all the days to come. They have accepted a responsibility that few would ever accept: the care for the souls of others. I know the work is demanding, for I add my own demands to those of others. I know the outward rewards are few, for our budgets are limited. Yet still they carry on, bright spots shining in the midst of dark humanity.

Wherever possible, make their loads lighter; where that is impossible, make their shoulders strong. Be with them throughout the long days and sleepless nights, and assure them that their work is not in vain.

2. The Fruitful Congregation

The harvest truly is great,
but the labourers are few:
pray ye therefore the Lord of the harvest,
that he would send forth labourers
into his harvest.
Luke 10:2

No fruitful congregation can be the result of one person's work, no matter how dedicated that person may be. Every leader must have followers, or who is there to be led? I thank You for all those in the church who spend their time and energy doing Your work. Remind them that their contributions are both needed and appreciated, especially when I begin to take their work for granted.

At the same time, show me if I am holding back from personally playing a part in Your harvest. My time and talents may seem limited, but You know how to use me, if only I am open to Your calling. I want our congregation to be fruitful.

3. LEADERS' BLESSING

I am the door of the sheep. . . .
By me if any man enter in,
he shall be saved,
and shall go in and out,
and find pasture.
JOHN 10:7, 9

Only leaders who know and follow You can point the way to salvation. I pray that You would bless those godly leaders in my life who have pointed me to You. They've inspired and encouraged me to grow in knowledge of You and share the message of Your good news. I could never give them a gift that could repay their efforts.

Touch these men and women who have turned me in the right direction. When they face discouragement, lift them up. When they need a word of encouragement, let my lips be quick to offer it.

4. Teaching

Whosoever therefore shall break one
of these least commandments,
and shall teach men so,
he shall be called the least
in the kingdom of heaven:
but whosoever shall do and teach them,
the same shall be called great
in the kingdom of heaven.
MATTHEW 5:19

Thank You, Lord God, for the faithful pastor You have brought to me. From him, I have learned how You want me to live. His truth-filled preaching has blessed many lives, and I recognize that he deserves Your blessings in heaven.

Give my pastor wisdom in teaching Your Word as You would have it taught. As he studies the Scriptures, may Your wisdom and Spirit guide him. Keep him faithful to You, even in hardships and doubts. I ask that You would pour out Your blessings on this one who has so often blessed me.

1. Two Types of Patience

For what glory is it, if,
when ye be buffeted for your faults,
ye shall take it patiently?
but if, when ye do well,
and suffer for it,
ye take it patiently,
this is acceptable with God.
1 Peter 2:20

Father, I find it "just" when I suffer for my faults, so I bear it with patience. But You remind me that this type of patience brings no one any glory; I just got what I deserved.

Other times, though, I find myself suffering because I did the right thing, and it brought me only trouble. Now I have good reason to complain, and my patience under suffering becomes a virtue that glorifies You. Teach me the difference between these two types of patience, loving Father. Protect me when my work for You causes me pain, and help me to bear it for Your sake.

2. Waiting for the Promise

For ye have need of patience, that,
after ye have done the will of God,
ye might receive the promise.
Hebrews 10:36

I love Your promises, Father, and rush to claim every one, like a child at an Easter egg hunt. Sometimes I get the cart before the horse and claim a promise before I do Your will, which may explain why I don't always see the promise fulfilled. But even when I do Your will, the promise may seem to take forever, and I grow impatient.

Remind me that my view of time is not the same as Yours. A promise is not like a grocery-store coupon I can cash in at my pleasure. I receive Your blessings in Your good time, and the grace with which I wait for them shows others a lot about me—and about You. Make me a good witness, Father.

3. The Second Coming

Be patient therefore, brethren,
unto the coming of the Lord. . . .
Stablish your hearts:
for the coming of the Lord draweth nigh.
James 5:7–8

Sometimes, Lord, when trials surround me, I wish You would come this very minute. Even when I feel less pressure, I look forward to being at home in You. But You have another plan: You're teaching me to remain firm in the middle of struggles. It's not a lesson I enjoy, but it's one I know I need.

I want to get the benefit of patience, Lord, without the struggles. Change my heart to wait on You quietly and without complaint, so that I will be ready for Your coming.

4. ENDURANCE

But he that shall endure unto the end,
the same shall be saved.
MATTHEW 24:13

Lord, I must admit that words like *patience* and *endurance* aren't my favorites. They make me think of gritting my teeth and bearing up under troubles—and I never look forward to troubles.

Give me Your vision of patience and endurance, Jesus. You came to earth and bore my sins, when heaven was Your rightful home. You endured much on earth so that I could relate to You. Help me see the value in patiently enduring hardship. I look forward with joy to eternity with You. Strengthen me, Lord, to be patient until that day.

1. A Prayer for Those in Need

Blessed is he that considereth the poor:
the LORD *will deliver him in time of trouble.*
PSALM 41:1

Father, today I pray for those who are struggling with poverty, those in my own community and throughout the world. Let me not fall into the trap of considering the poor as different from myself, for You know how rapidly fortunes can change and the wealthiest can fall into difficulty. Help me be generous with both my donations and my efforts to help those in need. The little I can contribute seems ineffective, but You will multiply it because I am Your child and precious in Your sight.

2. God's Love for the Poor

He will regard the prayer of the destitute,
and not despise their prayer.
Psalm 102:17

Lord, I admit I do not always treat the poor with the same consideration I give to others. I tend to step around them, to keep a distance between myself and the needy, as if poverty were somehow catching. I do so because I know that, except for Your grace, I could well be in the same situation. The poor frighten me not because of who or what they are but because of what I know I could become.

I know that You have a special regard for the poor; You always hear their prayers and You are their friend when others pass by them. Be their comfort, their hope for the future, the one constant presence they can count on when I fail them.

3. The Poor and Evildoers

Sing unto the LORD,
praise ye the LORD:
for he hath delivered the soul
of the poor from the hand of evildoers.
JEREMIAH 20:13

How much wealth I have on earth doesn't matter to You, Lord, for You already own the entire earth. Whatever my income, Your concern is for my soul.

I praise You that even the person with no money or possessions can trust in You. Your wisdom, which does not judge by outward appearances, sees to the heart and saves the soul of the one who turns to You. Though the wicked may threaten, none can harm the soul that belongs to You.

Thank You for Your care for each of Your children. No matter what I own, turn me to You for provision for my body and soul.

4. Spiritual Poverty

Blessed are the poor in spirit:
for theirs is the kingdom of heaven.
Matthew 5:3

Being poor in spirit doesn't seem like an attractive thing, Lord. It's not something I'd think to covet. But if I'd never realized how needy I was, I'd never have come to You with my sins. Thank You for showing me my poverty and promising me Your kingdom in return for my sin.

As I grow in faith, I'm often tempted to ignore my poverty and become proud in the changes You've brought into my life. I start to take credit for things You've done. Remind me then of my need for You, the source of my spiritual riches. Without You, I am poor, yet You offer me the riches of heaven. I am blessed indeed.

1. Prisons Without Bars

Bring my soul out of prison,
that I may praise thy name:
the righteous shall compass me about;
for thou shalt deal bountifully with me.
Psalm 142:7

Father, we are all prisoners of something. I may not be behind bars, but neither am I totally free. Whether I am a prisoner of sin, a prisoner of fear, a prisoner of poverty, or a prisoner of poor health, I ask You to hear my prayer and give me Your perfect freedom.

Let my brothers and sisters give me guidance and support as I struggle with my personal prison, showing me the way to freedom through their love and compassion. Then, when I am free, let me give the same help to others who need my encouragement in their struggles.

2. Judgment Is Yours

Let the sighing of the prisoner
come before thee;
according to the greatness of
thy power preserve thou those
that are appointed to die.
Psalm 79:11

Father, I ask You to be with those who are in prison for whatever cause. Some of them may be innocent martyrs in foreign lands; others have broken the law and are imprisoned in their own country; still others will suffer death for their crimes.

I do not condone those who are justly imprisoned, but I still owe them brotherly love and compassion, knowing You have the power to turn their lives around. Judgment is Yours, not mine, to make. Hear their prayers and offer them Your justice when ours fails. Be with them all in their despair, and give them hope.

3. God's Power

But thus saith the Lord,
Even the captives of the mighty
shall be taken away,
and the prey of the terrible shall be delivered:
for I will contend with him
that contendeth with thee,
and I will save thy children.
Isaiah 49:25

No matter what power attacks me, Lord, and seeks to imprison me, it holds no sway over me. When I am right with You, no authority, not even Satan, can place me beyond Your deliverance.

Thank You, Lord, for being my protector, no matter what situation I find myself in. Whether I become a political prisoner or am tied hand and foot by sin, I can trust in Your deliverance as I continue in Your love.

Deliver me, Lord, from all that binds me. I cannot free myself.

4. God's Rescue

The Lord thy God will turn thy captivity,
and have compassion upon thee,
and will return and gather thee
from all the nations,
whither the Lord thy God hath scattered thee.
If any of thine be driven out unto
the outmost parts of heaven,
from thence will the Lord thy God gather thee,
and from thence will he fetch thee.
Deuteronomy 30:3–4

Wherever I go, I cannot separate myself from Your Spirit, Lord. No corner of the earth is far from You, and no sin or earthly power can place me out of Your reach.

I need You to rescue me. No matter what I've done, You can still reach me. Draw me near to You through Your Spirit's power.

1. God's Never-Failing Mercy

But if the wicked will turn from
all his sins that he hath committed,
and keep all my statutes,
and do that which is lawful and right,
he shall surely live, he shall not die.
Ezekiel 18:21

Father, I know that on my own I am incapable of keeping Your law perfectly, but Your mercy never ends, and Your justice never fails. You know my soul intimately and welcome me with joy every time I repent and turn back to You.

Have mercy upon me, merciful Father. Pour Your Spirit down on me, bringing me comfort on the worst of my days. Remind me that You will never let me go far from Your side, for You desire my presence even more than I desire Yours. You will go to any length to save me.

2. The Company of Sinners

For I am not come to call the righteous,
but sinners to repentance.
Matthew 9:13

Father, examine the way I use my time in Your service. Am I too comfortable? Do I spend my time in fellowship with other believers because it is pleasant and safe, or do I risk the company of sinners? Who needs me most, my neighbor in the pew or my brother and sister in need of repentance and forgiveness? How can I be more effective in my outreach and missionary work?

Your Son showed me by example how I should be spending my time. Give me the strength and courage to make the hard choices, to go where I am needed, to minister to those seemingly beyond help—to risk the company of sinners.

3. Brokenhearted

The Lord is nigh unto them
that are of a broken heart;
and saveth such as be
of a contrite spirit.
Psalm 34:18

Lord, my heart feels broken. Life hasn't turned out the way I expected, and I feel worn and overwhelmed.

I confess I haven't followed Your will, and my will has not turned out well. Please forgive me, Lord, and make my life new. Turn my heart from its self-centered path onto one focused on You.

Praise You, Lord, for Your love that saves me. Thank You for caring for my soul.

4. Healing

He healeth the broken in heart,
and bindeth up their wounds.
Psalm 147:3

Thank You, Lord, for healing me. I came to You in sin, and You cleansed me. My sore heart found rest in You, and my spiritual cuts and bruises became whole under Your hand.

But this world still bruises and breaks me, Lord. When I fall into sin again, it cuts my soul. Every moment of my life, I need Your healing touch. Place Your hand on me this day.

I look forward to the day when You provide Your complete healing in eternity. I want to be entirely whole, Lord God. But until then, I trust in You to heal all my hurts. Each day I come to You for strength.

1. The Sting of Reproach

Blessed are ye, when men shall hate you,
and when they shall separate you from their company,
and shall reproach you,
and cast out your name as evil,
for the Son of man's sake.
Luke 6:22

The sting of reproach frightens me, Lord, in whatever form it comes upon me. When I do Your work, I am vulnerable. Some will mock me and my beliefs, others will consider me dangerous, maybe even slightly crazy, or at least out of touch with modern life. Such experiences will make me hold back when I know I should move forward boldly. Reproach hurts; I will do almost anything to avoid it.

Make me strong when I am weak; give me courage when I am afraid. If reproach comes to me, teach me how to deal with it in a godly manner for the sake of Your glory.

2. The Desolation of Reproach

Thou hast known my reproach,
and my shame, and my dishonour:
mine adversaries are all before thee.
Psalm 69:19

When I suffer for You, Lord, I experience such desolation that it's almost unbearable. Why do people avoid my company when I tell them I am a committed Christian? Am I coming on too strong? Do I seem critical instead of loving? I search for faults in myself that may explain the actions of others. Most of all, I am lonely.

Remind me in these times that I am not alone, that You know exactly how I feel because You went through it, all the way to the cross. My reproach is nothing compared to what You suffered for me. Perhaps the mockery of others can even be useful. If I react to it with forgiveness and love, those who mock me may see a bit of Your glory shining through me.

3. God's Glory

If ye be reproached for the
name of Christ, happy are ye;
for the spirit of glory
and of God resteth upon you:
on their part he is evil spoken of,
but on your part he is glorified.
1 Peter 4:14

When others speak ill of me because I tell them of Your love, I glorify You, Lord. What an amazing promise! To be glorified for my stand for You is a blessing.

But I must admit I don't often think of it as a blessing. I'm more likely to agree with people than take a firm stand against them. It's not pleasant being criticized and condemned.

Remind me, Father, that no one on earth gives the final condemnation. Though people may heap harsh words or actions on me, they only have temporal power. Yours is the final opinion—the one that really counts.

4. Fear of Reproach

Hearken unto me,
ye that know righteousness,
the people in whose heart is my law;
fear ye not the reproach of men,
neither be ye afraid of their revilings.
Isaiah 51:7

Am I listening to You, Lord—or to the criticism of those who reproach me? Am I avoiding doing Your will and doing right, so that I do not earn their hard words?

If I obey You, Father God, I will have nothing to fear from my critics. When my life follows Your commandments, righteous people will soon see that those who revile me have an agenda to fulfill and that I have not done wrong.

Fill my ears with Your words, Lord God, so I won't hear the complaints of those who hate You.

1. God's Provision

The young lions do lack,
and suffer hunger:
but they that seek the Lord
shall not want any good thing.
Psalm 34:10

Gracious Lord, thank You for Your faithfulness in providing for those who follow Your way righteously. I know every creature of this earth will face difficult times sooner or later. Even the strong may go hungry, but You are faithful to meet my needs.

When You have blessed me by Your provision, remind me to share the blessing with others less fortunate than I am, so they will have the strength to continue in the faith through my generosity. Help them see that Your provision may come in many forms, from many sources, but every good thing comes from You.

2. The Fruit of Righteousness

Say ye to the righteous,
that it shall be well with him:
for they shall eat the fruit of their doings.
Isaiah 3:10

I do Your work expecting no material reward, Father. Those I help often have nothing to give in return, and if they did, I would not want to take it from their families. My reward comes from the giving itself, and even when the giving can be painful, I continue for Your sake.

Although I ask nothing for my acts of conscience, You are quick to bless me. When I give honesty, I am treated honestly. When I give love, I am loved. When I provide justice, others are just with me. When I ask for nothing, You give me everything I could ever hope for and will never deserve.

3. Glorifying God

But he that glorieth,
let him glory in the Lord.
For not he that
commendeth himself is approved,
but whom the Lord commendeth.
2 Corinthians 10:17–18

I can't look good in Your eyes, Lord, by glorifying myself. When I try to do that, I only become self-righteous. Forgive me for my tendency to put myself before You.

But thank You that I can glory in Your righteousness. How wonderful are Your moral laws and the commendation You give when I do Your will.

May I only seek to lift You up, Lord. May my words tell of Your goodness instead of my own. When I hear Your words of commendation, they will still only reflect Your glory.

4. When Doing Right Goes Wrong

For the Lord *knoweth*
the way of the righteous:
but the way of the ungodly shall perish.
Psalm 1:6

Sometimes, Lord, even doing right gets me into trouble. My heart seemed to be in the right place, but things haven't worked out the way I expected. The good I thought would happen has turned sour.

Thank You, Jesus, that even this situation is not out of Your hands. You knew what would happen even from the start, and the results are under Your control.

I know I can trust You to make all things right, even if it takes some time. Whatever happens, make me a good testimony to Your love.

1. The Salvation of All

For this is good and acceptable
in the sight of God our Saviour;
who will have all men to be saved,
and to come unto the knowledge of the truth.
1 Timothy 2:3–4

Loving Father, only You know what is in a person's heart; only You are able to judge and save. You say it is Your desire that all should be saved and know Your truth, that through Your Son You have made salvation available to me if I but ask for it. I thank You for this greatest blessing of all.

Remind me that I am not Your gatekeeper or Your judge. My task is to spread the joyful gospel to all, to believe You will make my efforts fruitful, and never to stand in the way of another's salvation. Open my heart, show me where I am needed, and I will trust the rest to You.

2. The Gift of Salvation

Not by works of righteousness
which we have done,
but according to his mercy
he saved us, by the washing of regeneration,
and renewing of the Holy Ghost.
Titus 3:5

Salvation cannot be earned; grace cannot be demanded as payment for my services. No matter how I strive to live in righteousness, I will always fall short of Your standards. You know this, gracious Father; otherwise You would not have sent Your Son for the salvation of all who claim His name.

But You did send Him, and the Holy Ghost is with me today because of my neediness. Thank You for making my perfection possible in the life to come. By myself, I would certainly fail. With You, anything is possible.

3. New Life

Therefore if any man be in Christ,
he is a new creature:
old things are passed away;
behold, all things are become new.
2 Corinthians 5:17

Sometimes I feel so clean, Lord, when I've confessed sin and put it far behind me. Then I know the truth of this verse. Other times, even when I'm serving You, I feel dull and slightly used.

Thank You that Your salvation reaches beyond my feelings. It doesn't matter how I feel. When sin causes me to feel doubt or dullness, You don't toss me out of Your kingdom, but call me to new faith. I need You to renew me constantly.

Make me new again this day.

4. Seeking God

The LORD is with you,
while ye be with him;
and if ye seek him,
he will be found of you;
but if ye forsake him,
he will forsake you.
2 CHRONICLES 15:2

Lord, You showed me Your wonderful salvation, using Your people to draw me to Your love. When I knew nothing of You, You prepared a way for me to accept You.

How can I repay Your gift of freedom from sin? I own nothing valuable enough to repay the life of Your Son. Even if I give You each and every day of the rest of my life, the gift would be too small.

But take my life. Keep me strong in You: Forsaking You would be too painful a thing to imagine. My life is Yours, Father. May I honor You all my days.

1. A Prayer of Faith

And the prayer of faith shall save the sick,
and the Lord shall raise him up;
and if he have committed sins,
they shall be forgiven him.
James 5:15

Father, today I pray for the sick among us, those whom medicine has failed, those whose only hope remains in Your compassion and power. You may or may not choose to heal those I lift up to You, but I know You have the power, if healing is in Your will.

I ask You to cleanse their souls as well as their bodies, to keep them strong in the faith no matter what befalls them, and to be a source of comfort to those who love them. Stand by them all in their time of suffering, wrap them in Your arms of love, and if You choose, heal their bodies.

2. A Prayer for Health Workers

For I will restore health unto thee,
and I will heal thee of thy wounds,
saith the Lord.
Jeremiah 30:17

Bless those who work in the health sciences, focusing all their efforts and lives on keeping me well or returning me to health. Their job is never ending, often not properly rewarded or acknowledged. Give them the strength and wisdom they need to continue; reward them for their efforts with peace of mind in emotional times. Be their strength and their comfort forever.

3. Healed by Jesus

But he was wounded for our transgressions,
he was bruised for our iniquities;
the chastisement of our peace was upon him;
and with his stripes we are healed.
Isaiah 53:5

Lord, I do not even know how many times You have already restored my health. I may have never seen or understood many of Your actions, and I may often credit others for what was actually Your healing and preservation. But I know You are always with me, and I thank You for Your protection.

Father God, whether it's a physical sickness or a spiritual one, You have promised I have healing in Jesus. No illness is beyond Your power, Lord. When I suffer from sin or physical pain, keep me mindful that Your hand is still on me. May each trial strengthen me spiritually and draw me nearer to You. Ultimately, I will experience Your healing—here or in heaven.

Keep me mindful of the price Your Son paid so I could enjoy a healthy relationship with You. Let my trust in You never fail.

4. Protection

Thou shalt not bow down to their gods,
nor serve them, nor do after their works. . . .
And ye shall serve the LORD your God,
and he shall bless thy bread,
and thy water;
and I will take sickness away
from the midst of thee.
EXODUS 23:24–25

Service to You may have a price, Lord, but it also offers a huge benefit. Thank You for caring for my every need and keeping at bay the things that would hurt me.

I cannot know how many physical and spiritual illnesses I have avoided by obeying You, but I have seen the blessing of sickness healed, spirits cleansed, and provision made for my daily well-being.

Rule among us, Lord. I know that following You is the best way to live and the only way You are glorified. Live in my heart today.

1. Avoiding Sin

Neither yield ye your members
as instruments of unrighteousness unto sin:
but yield yourselves unto God,
as those that are alive from the dead,
and your members as instruments
of righteousness unto God.
For sin shall not have dominion over you:
for ye are not under the law,
but under grace.
Romans 6:13–14

The fight against sin is a serious struggle, Lord, one I face every day. Thank You for promising that as I wage war against sin, I am not under its dominion. Your grace frees me from my enemy, giving me the ability to be successful. I can choose not to follow Satan and to yield myself to Your will.

When Satan tempts me, pour out Your grace on me. Hold me firm in Your grasp and empower me to do Your will. This battle can only be won in Your name.

2. God's Covenant

This is the covenant
that I will make with them
after those days, saith the Lord,
I will put my laws into their hearts,
and in their minds will I write them;
and their sins and iniquities
will I remember no more.
Hebrews 10:16–17

You have written Your law in my heart and mind, Lord, and separated me from sin. Even when I fail You, You do not remember that sin, but consider me sanctified, because of Your Son.

How little I deserve Your covenant, Lord, yet without it I would have no way of fighting against sin. Even my best efforts at doing right would go all wrong.

Thank You for Your cleansing, which has touched my heart and mind. May my entire being focus on You no matter what goes on in the world around me.

3. Repentance

If we confess our sins,
he is faithful and just
to forgive us our sins,
and to cleanse us from
all unrighteousness.
1 John 1:9

From the days when I first came to know You, O God, I believed Your promise that forgiveness required only simple, honest confession and repentance.

But how my soul struggles to daily frame those words of repentance. Willfulness and rebellion make my confessions stick in my throat. Though I ache to admit my faults, sin holds me back.

Free me, Savior, to open my soul to You. May my heart show me my error and prompt me to quickly seek pardon. Cleanse me from all sin and glorify Yourself in my life.

4. Salvation

So Christ was once offered
to bear the sins of many;
and unto them that look for him
shall he appear the second time
without sin unto salvation.
HEBREWS 9:28

How expectantly I wait for You, Jesus. I long to shed the sin that still hangs on to my soul as I wait here on earth. Though I know Your salvation is working in my life, my own sin seeks to control me.

What freedom from sin You have already given me—but how much more sin needs to be removed from me! As I trust in You, I know You are faithful to cleanse my life more each day.

I trust in Your promise and look for the day when You return, Jesus. I long to be with You.

1. My Thankfulness

Every man also to whom
God hath given riches and wealth,
and hath given him power to eat thereof,
and to take his portion,
and to rejoice in his labour;
this is the gift of God.
Ecclesiastes 5:19

It is truly a blessing when I am able to enjoy my work and the profits of that work, Father. While I may not be rich, I have much more than the rest of the world, and You allow me pleasures that are unknown to many.

When I turn from thankfulness and begin to desire some of the things I do not have, remind me of the millions who suffer in poverty every day, no matter how hard they work. Remind me of Your blessings that have little to do with wealth: love, peace, good health, and the work of the Spirit in my life. Remind me of the great cost of my salvation, and let me praise You forever.

2. My Blessings

And all these blessings shall come on thee,
and overtake thee,
if thou shalt hearken unto the voice
of the Lord *thy God.*
Blessed shalt thou be in the city,
and blessed shalt thou be in the field.
Blessed shall be the fruit of thy body,
and the fruit of thy ground,
and the fruit of thy cattle,
the increase of thy kine,
and the flocks of thy sheep.
Blessed shall be thy basket and thy store.
Blessed shalt thou be when thou comest in,
and blessed shalt thou be when thou goest out.
Deuteronomy 28:2–6

Father, I thank You for Your promises and provision. You touch my life in every way, never denying me that which I truly need, helping me flourish. Without You, I would surely fail, but with You, anything is possible for me.

3. My Stewardship

The LORD shall open
unto thee his good treasure,
the heaven to give the rain
unto thy land in his season,
and to bless all the work of thine hand.
DEUTERONOMY 28:12

Father, the world abounds with Your blessings: fertile soil, nourishing rain, the warmth of the sun, the cooling breezes. Everything I need is given to me as a gift, and I am free to use it all.

You have given me stewardship of this world, but I have often failed in my responsibilities. I have depleted the soil, fouled the rivers and seas, polluted the air, and exterminated Your creatures in my haste to make myself rich. Forgive me these trespasses against Your creation, Father. Show me where I have done wrong. Teach me how to correct my selfish acts and live in harmony with Your precious world. When I do, that will be the true measure of my success.

4. My Savior

Better is the poor that walketh
in his uprightness,
than he that is perverse in his ways,
though he be rich.
Proverbs 28:6

Father, I tend to listen to the advice of the successful, not the poor. No one would think of going to a poor man for financial advice—he has no power. If he did, he would be rich, wouldn't he? I think the rich must have knowledge I do not have, and if I follow their advice, I, too, may know success.

But You sent Your Son as a humble man, a man without power or riches as the world counts power and riches. Help me see the wisdom of that act, and remind me that Your Son spent most of His ministry among the powerless, suffering the death of a criminal for my sake.

1. Consolation

And our hope of you is stedfast, knowing, that as ye are partakers of the sufferings, so shall ye be also of the consolation.
2 Corinthians 1:7

I know I am allotted a certain amount of suffering in this world, whether it is suffering for Your sake or just the common suffering related to being human. People I love die; supporting my family is hard or impossible; and in the end, I must come to grips with my own mortality.

But I do not let suffering overcome me or totally overshadow the joys of life, for I know You are with me in my deepest need, carrying me through the hard times safely to the other side.

Please be with those who are suffering today, Father. Give them the hope to carry on, knowing the victory is theirs through Christ our Lord.

2. Exceeding Joy

Beloved, think it not strange concerning
the fiery trial which is to try you,
as though some strange thing
happened unto you:
but rejoice, inasmuch as ye are
partakers of Christ's sufferings;
that, when his glory shall be revealed,
ye may be glad also with exceeding joy.
1 Peter 4:12–13

My suffering will never approach Yours, Lord. You had power and knowledge beyond understanding, yet You willingly gave them up for my sake, dying a human death to serve as my example and salvation. I cannot imagine everything You sacrificed for me, but I thank You from the bottom of my heart.

When Your glory is revealed at the end, I pray that I might share Your joy, as You have shared my sufferings. The suffering of this life will be as nothing compared to the joy I will feel then.

3. Comfort

Blessed be. . .the God of all comfort;
who comforteth us in all our tribulation,
that we may be able to comfort them
which are in any trouble,
by the comfort wherewith
we ourselves are comforted of God.
2 Corinthians 1:3–4

What a blessing it is, Lord, to experience comfort that comes directly from Your heart. No matter what my troubles, Your peace reaches the hurting places within me.

Help me to pass comfort on to those who are also in need. Open my heart to Your wisdom and gentleness, and let the light of compassion burn brightly in my life because of the solace I have received.

4. Christian Suffering

For unto you it is given
in the behalf of Christ,
not only to believe on him,
but also to suffer for his sake.
PHILIPPIANS 1:29

According to Your promises, Lord, suffering is part of the Christian experience. It's not one I enjoy, but to know You more completely, I must experience suffering. If I trust You and have lived out my commitment faithfully, I need not worry about suffering and ask where it comes from. Those who trust in You need have no fear.

Help me to deal with suffering in a way that draws others to You and brings glory to Your name. I want to be faithful in all things.

1. The Crown of Life

Blessed is the man that endureth temptation:
for when he is tried,
he shall receive the crown of life,
which the Lord hath promised
to them that love him.
James 1:12

Lord, I am on the lookout for the big temptations of the Ten Commandments, and by and large I can avoid them because they are so obvious. It's the little pebbles on the road of life that worry me, that make me stumble and fear for my life with You.

You came to save me, to throw my sin to the bottom of the seas, to make me pure enough to receive the crown of life and be with You for eternity. My duty is to love You; my sins I leave for You to handle because I cannot. I am not afraid.

2. No Problem Too Small

The Lord knoweth how to
deliver the godly out of temptations.
2 Peter 2:9

Thank You, Lord, for Your active part in delivering me from temptation. I cannot save myself from human weakness, no matter how hard I try, but You can and will answer my calls for help.

Remind me that no problem is too small to bring to You in prayer; there is no such thing as a small temptation in Your eyes. Anything that might separate me from You is serious, worthy of Your attention and care. Only You know how to deliver me, to make me fit to be called a child of God.

3. God's Faithfulness

There hath no temptation taken you
but such as is common to man:
but God is faithful,
who will not suffer you to be tempted
above that ye are able;
but will with the temptation
also make a way to escape,
that ye may be able to bear it.
1 Corinthians 10:13

How glad I am that You gave me this promise, Lord. Even when temptation becomes sharp and compelling, I know You have provided a way out. If I flee from sin, You will lead me into freedom.

Help me avoid temptation when it is still very small, Lord. I don't want to allow things into my life that could draw me away from You.

Thank You for being an escape hatch that is constantly available. Don't let my pride keep me from freedom.

4. JESUS' GRACE

For we have not an high priest
which cannot be touched with
the feeling of our infirmities;
but was in all points tempted like as we are, yet without sin.
Let us therefore come boldly unto the throne of grace,
that we may obtain mercy,
and find grace to help in time of need.
HEBREWS 4:15–16

Thank You, Jesus, for coming to earth, so that You could feel my hurts and temptations. You are not some distant, unfeeling God who criticizes me without knowing what I face. You cared for me so deeply, You came to be like me.

Help me to bring my temptations and sins to You. Cleanse my heart and mind as I confess to You. I desperately need Your mercy. Fill my life with Your grace, that I may share it with the world.

1. Taking the Wrong Path

Trust in the LORD with all thine heart;
and lean not unto thine own understanding.
In all thy ways acknowledge him,
and he shall direct thy paths.
PROVERBS 3:5–6

It is hard for me not to take matters into my own hands, Lord, especially when things are going wrong for me and I can see no sign of Your direction. I believe I know my own needs; I think I know what must be done, so I race ahead of You, only to find I have taken the wrong path and I'm in even deeper trouble than ever.

Teach me to rely on You, not on my own understanding. I trust You totally. You are the only map I need if I will just be patient and wait for Your direction. Lead me, Lord.

2. "Don't Be Afraid"

Fear not, little flock;
for it is your Father's good pleasure
to give you the kingdom.
Luke 12:32

Don't be afraid. How many times have I said that to my children? I know that nightmares are not real and not every barking dog bites. I know that eating spinach is not fatal and that even the darkest night is followed by a bright sunrise. Yet still they have fears I cannot ease.

I come to You like the child I am, Father, still afraid of the dark that lingers in my mind. You take great pleasure in me, anxious to give me Your kingdom, but my fears hold me back. Help me to trust in Your love the way my children trust in mine, for only then will I experience the joyful life You have designed me to live.

3. Worldly Cares

Therefore take no thought,
saying, What shall we eat?
or, What shall we drink? or,
Wherewithal shall we be clothed? . . .
for your heavenly Father knoweth
that ye have need of all these things.
Matthew 6:31–32

You sent Your disciples out into the world with nothing but Your teaching, Lord, confident that their physical needs would be met if they sought the kingdom of God and God's righteousness, depending on the Father for everything else. To Your glory. . .that's exactly how they lived the remainder of their lives.

I wish my faith were that strong. I wish I could leave my concerns behind and dedicate my life to Your work. Forgive me my worldly attachments and anxieties. Help me seek Your kingdom so I may live as a good example of Your never-failing care and concern.

4. Mount Zion

They that trust in the LORD
shall be as mount Zion,
which cannot be removed,
but abideth for ever.
As the mountains are round about Jerusalem,
so the LORD is round about his people
from henceforth even for ever.
PSALM 125:1–2

I come to You seeking a safe haven, Father, a town nestled in a mountain chain, safe from any attack from the outside world. I come seeking peace and the freedom to follow Your way. Of course I know there is no such place, geographically speaking; Jerusalem fell often, mountains or not.

What I seek is Your presence, Father. I trust in You, and You have promised to be with me forever, surrounding me with Your sheltering arms. I seek to be Your mountain—faithful forever, secure in Your love, unmovable in times of peril.

1. Waiting at the Door

I am come a light into the world,
that whosoever believeth on me
should not abide in darkness.
John 12:46

Lord, so many people stumble through life in darkness, afraid of what they might touch in the blackness, of what they might become. They have no sense of direction and no peace in their lives; only anger and fear keep them moving.

You stand outside the door, life-giving light in Your presence, if only they would turn the key and welcome You. You will wait there forever, if need be, eternally patient and loving. I pray they will hear You knocking on their hearts; may they gather up their courage and answer Your call, for You offer them light, guidance, and nothing less than salvation itself.

2. Contact with the Unsaved

Blessed is the man that walketh
not in the counsel of the ungodly,
nor standeth in the way of sinners,
nor sitteth in the seat of the scornful.

Psalm 1:1

You promise to bless me, Lord, when I turn away from constant contact with evil people. Help me glorify You through my friendships and associations.

But continue to keep my heart burning to reach those souls who do not know You. May my prayers remain constant, asking that Your Spirit would touch the souls of the unsaved around me. My prayers can still reach out to those with whom I do not walk, stand, or sit.

Turn their lives around, just as You have mine.

3. Enemies of God

Behold, they shall surely gather together,
but not by me:
whosoever shall gather together
against thee shall fall for thy sake.
ISAIAH 54:15

When my enemies attack me, they may gather against me because they hate You, Lord. But as they surround me, I can be certain I do not stand alone. You stand beside me, and the end is certain: You have promised that all who fight against You will eventually fall.

The battle is not mine, so I need not viciously attack another. As I firmly stand on Your Word and do what is right, You will ultimately bring victory. May I show Your love to those who gather against me. Open their eyes to know You, too.

4. CHRISTIAN FEARLESSNESS

So that we may boldly say,
The Lord is my helper,
and I will not fear
what man shall do unto me.
HEBREWS 13:6

When my enemies stand before me, Lord, fear is the first emotion that covers me. Uncertain about the future, I begin to worry about the things I could lose to these people.

Your promise tells me I have nothing to fear. What can I lose that is not already in Your hand? What can I lose that is not already in Your control? With Your help, I am secure and guarded against every attack.

Thank You for Your protection. Keep me from fear and strengthen my trust in You.

1. Blessings of Wisdom

For God giveth to a man
that is good in his sight wisdom,
and knowledge, and joy.
Ecclesiastes 2:26

When I came to You, Lord, I expected forgiveness for my sins, but You have offered so much more! Not only do You give me the freedom from wrongdoing that I was seeking, You also give me three wonderful ways to live well and glorify You. Thank You for Your wisdom, thank You for the knowledge of how to live in Your sight, and thank You for the joy that floods my soul. Wisdom, knowledge, and joy are the "bumper crop" that accompanies forgiveness, an unexpected blessing to my soul. Your generous gifts are beyond compare.

Teach me to live in Your wisdom, knowledge, and joy. May they bless me, my family, and even the entire world around me.

2. My Continual Source

I will bless the Lord,
who hath given me counsel:
my reins also instruct me
in the night seasons.
Psalm 16:7

No matter what the time of day or condition of my life, You give me wise counsel, Father God. Nothing but my own willfulness and doubt can keep me from Your wisdom. You are always willing to show me the best action to take, and You direct my thoughts.

Thank You for being available to me in the nighttime hours—or the nights of my soul. When darkness would cover me, You still shine brightly, lighting my life with truth.

Help me to walk in Your truth every hour of my days.

3. Understanding

Evil men understand not judgment:
but they that seek the LORD
understand all things.
PROVERBS 28:5

I am glad to be in the court of the just judge who never fails to make a fair decision, Lord. You see into the hearts of people and judge rightly.

Thank You for sharing Your wisdom with me. Unlike those who rebel against You, God, You often let me realize the wisdom in Your rules and plans. I begin to see the design You have for ruling the world.

Rule my life, also. Your judgments are always wise.

4. Walking in Wisdom

And he will teach us of his ways,
and we will walk in his paths.
Isaiah 2:3

You have promised me that I can know Your ways and walk in them, Lord. What a blessing that is to me, for I cannot know You more closely unless I know how You want me to live and can follow in Your footsteps.

I may not always be sure of my path. But I can be sure of You; as I continue to seek Your way, You will lead me to the right goal.

You, Lord Jesus, are always my goal. You are the end of my path; my eternal reward is to live with You forever. Thank You that my way leads to Your eternal home.

1. Becoming Wise

Thou hast known the holy scriptures,
which are able to make thee wise
unto salvation through faith
which is in Christ Jesus.
All scripture is given by inspiration of God,
and is profitable for doctrine,
for reproof, for correction,
for instruction in righteousness.
2 Timothy 3:15–16

You offer me so much wisdom in Your Book, Lord. Not only have You used it to draw me to Your side in salvation, You provide me with a lifetime of insight for leading a life that glorifies You and makes me more like You.

I praise You for Your generous sharing of Yourself. Though I will never be as wise as You, knowing all things, You have graciously shared this part of Your nature. I am blessed by Your touch. May I live every moment by the light of Your Word and become righteous through knowledge of Your Son, Jesus Christ.

2. Eternal Life

Search the scriptures;
for in them ye think ye have eternal life:
and they are they which testify of me.
John 5:39

Father, eternal life comes no other way but by knowing Your Son, Jesus. Thank You for providing Your Word as a testimony to Him, for from it I learn the truth about Your love for me and the sin that separates me from You.

When questions arise in my heart or the hearts of those who do not believe in You, make me quick to search Your Word for the evidence of truth. Keep me daily in the Scriptures, so that I will always be ready to respond to doubt.

3. Power

For the word of God is quick, and powerful,
and sharper than any twoedged sword,
piercing even to the dividing
asunder of soul and spirit,
and of the joints and marrow,
and is a discerner of the thoughts
and intents of the heart.
Hebrews 4:12

Your Word is so much a part of You, Lord, that it pierces the deepest parts of my soul. What can I hide from You? You see even the intentions of my heart that I cannot understand.

Use Your Word to cleanse my heart and mind and make them conform to You. I need Your Word's power to cut out sin and make me whole and pure. Give me a desire to feed on it often.

Thank You for Your amazing Word. May I draw close to it, so that I may be close to You.

4. Spiritual Growth

As newborn babes,
desire the sincere milk of the word,
that ye may grow thereby.
1 Peter 2:2

You start me out as a baby in Your Word, Lord God, and teach me simple things—but You never separate me from my need for Your Word's truth and the growth it brings. I am never full grown in every aspect of my spiritual life.

Thank You for providing so much growth potential in Your Word. No matter what I need, the truth and wisdom that will touch my life and the lives of others are in its pages. Make Your truths real to me, Lord. I want to grow in You and reach out to a world in pain.

1. Honest Work

Study to be quiet,
and to do your own business,
and to work with your hands,
as we commanded you;
that ye may walk honestly toward
them that are without,
and that ye may have lack of nothing.
1 Thessalonians 4:11–12

Father, honest work may never make me rich in the things of this world, but it does provide for my family and give me a sense of accomplishment. What I have, I earned, stealing nothing from my neighbors and treating others fairly.

I thank You for my work and the opportunities it brings me. May others not so blessed find the jobs for which they are searching. May we all work in a manner that brings glory to You.

2. Slack Hands

He becometh poor
that dealeth with a slack hand:
but the hand of the diligent maketh rich.
Proverbs 10:4

It's so easy to fall prey to the "slack-hand syndrome," Lord. Sometimes I can do my work without ever engaging my brain. A job that was once a challenge is soon mastered, and I find myself growing bored and sloppy, cutting corners, giving less and less of myself.

Help me see these symptoms when they first appear and do something to change my work habits. Perhaps I need more responsibilities and challenges; perhaps a minor reality check is in order. I want to be known as a diligent worker, not someone with slack hands. Thank You for Your guidance, Lord.

3. Flourishing

He that trusteth
in his riches shall fall:
but the righteous
shall flourish as a branch.
Proverbs 11:28

In the workplace, it's hard to know who can be trusted and who cannot. Often I find that the modest employee is more trustworthy than the one who has all the money he needs and is resting on his laurels, making life difficult for everyone else.

Be my guide through the everyday maze at work. Give me the sense to see through pretense and recognize the truly competent workers around me, whatever their position on the corporate ladder. Let me choose my friends wisely, so I may flourish and contribute to the good of all.

4. My Lifeline

If any of you lack wisdom,
let him ask of God,
that giveth to all men liberally,
and upbraideth not;
and it shall be given him.
James 1:5

Lord, it's becoming more and more difficult to keep up with changes at work. Some of us, trained as pencil-and-paper workers, are now struggling to master complex computer programs in our "spare time," while still keeping up on our daily tasks. Others of us are going to college nights and weekends, leaving us no free time for our families.

I need Your wisdom, Lord. I'm in over my head, with only You as my lifeline. Help me with my priorities, both at home and at work. I want to be productive for Your glory, but I cannot do it on my own. Show me where I should change and how I can cope.

1. Lights in the Dark

Ye are the light of the world.
A city that is set
on an hill cannot be hid.
Matthew 5:14

You have changed my life, Lord. You have given me hope and lifted my burden from my back. In return, You ask only that I believe in You and live as the child of God You made me to be. I am different now, with the power to be the light of the world.

It's hard to be a beacon for the world, but that is what I am, even when I am reluctant to shine in public. Your love cannot be hidden; my joy cannot be concealed. Help me use my faith for the good of all, I pray. I am only a tiny speck of light in a dark world, but You promise that will be more than enough. All power and glory are Yours.

2. God's Messenger

For the grace of God that bringeth
salvation hath appeared to all men,
teaching us that,
denying ungodliness and worldly lusts,
we should live soberly,
righteously, and godly,
in this present world.
Titus 2:11–12

I try to be a good example of the Christian life, Lord, so that those in the world can look at me and perhaps begin to explore for themselves the faith that guides my life. I witness in various ways, depending on the gifts You have given me, because I want everyone to experience Your salvation.

I am not perfect. Others can always find fault with me, no matter how I live, but I am only Your messenger. Help me be a more effective witness for You, I pray.

3. Safety

And they shall no more be
a prey to the heathen,
neither shall the beast
of the land devour them;
but they shall dwell safely,
and none shall make them afraid.
Ezekiel 34:28

The world can be a scary place, Father. Without You, sin would devour me. But I have Your promise that, like a father, You provide me with safety and security. When I go out in Your name, obedient to Your will, I overcome many dangers.

Deliver me from the temptations of the world. Instead of focusing on the sin that invades my path, I want to see only You, Your vision for me, and the work that You have set before me. Keep me safe in You, Lord.

4. Separation

Behold, what manner of love
the Father hath bestowed upon us,
that we should be called the sons of God:
therefore the world knoweth us not,
because it knew him not.
1 John 3:1

The world doesn't understand what it means to love You, Lord. Sometimes I feel that truth very deeply when I witness to a friend and he looks at me as if I were strange. When a coworker just can't understand why doing right matters to me, I can feel awfully odd.

But I would rather be at Your side than on the side of all of those who don't love You. They don't know me because they don't know You, not because I am strange. Let the difference You make in my life shine out through me.